TWELVE STEPS TO

SPIRITUAL

AWAKENING

TWELVE STEPS TO

SPIRITUAL AWAKENING

ENLIGHTENMENT FOR EVERYONE

Herb K.

Cover design by Eileen Turpin

Publisher's Cataloging-in-Publication
K., Herb (1940 -   )   Twelve Steps To Spiritual Awakening: Enlightenment For Everyone
___ p. ___ cm.
    1.   Twelve-step programs
Library of Congress Control Number 2010927483
ISBN 978-0-9659672-4-2

Capizon Publishing   www.capizon.com
Printed in the USA
Third Printing March 2014

Printed on acid-free paper

DEDICATION

This book is dedicated to my wife, Mary.

None of any of this would have manifested without her incredible courage. Her decision for treatment for her alcoholism on February 10, 1984 said boldly that what was happening in our family was not all right. She was willing to sacrifice everything without any premonition that her action would redeem everything.

Table of Contents

Persian Proverb iii
Foreword v
Purpose of This Book vii
Definitions xii
Oxford Group Origins xiii

— ASLEEP —

In the Beginning ... Separation and Brokenness 1
Purpose 5
Preparation 7
Process 8

— AWAKENING —

Seeking Healing ... Instruction and Action 15
Chapter 1 Powerless: Name Our Sickness / Brokenness 19
Chapter 2 Power: Name the Healer 49
Chapter 3 Decision: to Have a Relationship With That Power 71
Chapter 4 Name Obstacles to This Relationship 85
Chapter 5 Reveal Obstacles to This Relationship 111
Chapter 6 Name Defects of Character 125
Chapter 7 Pray for Removal of Character Defects 139
Chapter 8 Name Harm Done to Others 153

Chapter 9   Make Amends: Personal Change and
              Reparation to Others   171
Chapter 10   Continue Emotional and Spiritual
              Growth   191
Chapter 11   Improve Our Conscious Contact With
              Power: Prayer and Meditation   205
Chapter 12   Enlarge Our Personal Spiritual Life:
              Service   231
Awakening: Summary of the Step Process   263

— STAYING AWAKE —

Journey of Freedom ... Union and Communion   269
Appendix A   Narcissistic Personality Disorder   295
Appendix B   Diagram of Pre-AA History   297
Appendix C   The Spiritual Journey Diagram   298
Appendix D   Dr. Carl Jung's letter to Bill Wilson   299
Appendix E   Inventory Worksheets (Step Four):
                 1. Resentment (Column Three)   301
                 2. Resentment (Column Four)   302
                 3. Fear Inventory   303
                 4. Sex Inventory   304
Appendix F   Character Defects Worksheet (Step Six)   305
Appendix G   Prayer and Meditation Practice (Step
              Eleven)   306
Bibliography   315
Acknowledgments   321
Twelve-Step Workbook and CDs/Tapes by Author   322

Persian Proverb

He who knows not
and knows not that he knows not
is a fool
— shun him.

He who knows not
and knows that he knows not
is a child
— teach him.

He who knows
and knows not that he knows
is asleep
— wake him.

He who knows
and knows that he knows
is wise
— follow him.

Foreword

This book guides us along a path of practical radicality. It is radical in that it goes to the very depths of all the Wisdom traditions of spiritual awakening, of realizing God's oneness with us in life itself.

At the same time, it is extremely practical. Instead of pursuing the description of that realization in philosophical, theological and abstract terms, it is always exploring this path to awakening experientially. With hands-on, actual experience it shows how each of us, in our own way and at our own pace, can keep opening ourselves and be taken ever deeper into this experience.

The significant character of this work is that it helps us to understand that the twelve-step program embodies this practical radicality. On the one hand, it sees that the alcoholic is in the grip of a disease that destroys life. On the other hand, it recognizes that by approaching that disease in this radical way we may discover that setting out on one's recovery is actually setting out on a practical path that inevitably leads to a spiritual awakening.

Then one discovers that one's alcoholism was just simply a more specific intense form of the universal dilemma of being addicted to our illusions and delusions about ourselves. Therefore, those reading this book who are in any of the Twelve Step fellowships will feel very comfortable with its spirit and accept its invitation to allow themselves to be taken deeper than they have been accustomed to going. This takes us closer to the original intention of the Co-founders of the initial Twelve Step program and its spiritual foundation.

Those of you who are not alcoholics, drug addicts, and/or members of the various twelve-step programs will easily recognize in the talk about stuck places, points of confusion, fear and reactivity, that we are actually in the domain of all of us as human beings in our brokenness.

Therefore, this book is essentially radical because it invites all of us, all humans dealing with the messiness of our lives, to discover and apply a specific process of healing. This book is eminently practical because it reveals a specific structure and methodology that guarantees healing through a spiritual awakening.

What's particularly at the heart of this book is a form of profound encouragement. The very thing we dread the most, the thing that hurts the most, that we're most ashamed of, that we're most afraid of, is that we don't have what it takes to rise above it. Yet, if deeply embraced with trust in God, this thing, this experience of powerlessness, ends up paradoxically being the pathway into this Oneness. That mystery, that surprising mystery, which we never suspected or expected, is the source of encouragement so badly needed today.

James Finley Ph.D.

Clinical Psychologist, Spiritual Director and Author

Purpose of This Book

*To describe a process of personal transformation
leading to spiritual awakening*

Sometime in the spring of 2005, just after re-reading Erick Fromm's "The Art of Loving," I was awakened at 2 a.m. with an overwhelming urge to write. It was well past sunrise when I set the pen down. The theme and outline of this book and most of the "Asleep" section were written.

In 2004 I wrote "Twelve-Step Guide to Using the Alcoholics Anonymous Big Book." It is a workbook capturing all the instructions I previously received from three different step guides who led me through the step process in 1988, 1991, and 1994.

For the last 14 years I have conducted workshops where participants travel this exact path through the steps, but on a group basis.

My 2 a.m. inspiration evolved into what I have interpreted as an invitation to describe and expand upon the content of my workshops. The "Awakening" section of this book describes the actual process of *working* the Twelve Steps (my first book documented the instructions only) and comments on my actual experience, confirming the results of my continuing personal transformation.

This current book represents my accumulated experiences of being led through the Twelve Steps as well as leading a number of individuals through the process I experienced.

History reveals many paths to spiritual awakening: an awareness or experience of the Divine that transforms an individual (instantly or over time). This enlightenment inspires a personal moral life and generates an authentic energy for altruistic service to individuals and community:

Hinduism	3500 bce*
Judaism	1300 bce
Buddhism	500 bce
Christianity	30 ce*
Islam	600 ce

Having personally tried many paths without much success, I am particularly grateful for being led to Twelve-Step spirituality. It is a unique distillation of history's many experiences, filtering out the jargon and dogma. It has no "shoulds" or "thou shalts"; but it does have definite suggestions, and even some "musts."

It differs from self-help programs by recognizing the futility of seeking and relying on human help. To effectively begin the Twelve-Step process a person must reach bottom— feel hopelessness and despair, while conceding personal powerlessness. The elevator moving down can stop at any floor. That becomes a person's "bottom."

The promise of completing all of the Twelve Steps is a spiritual awakening— we will be changed in the way we

---

* before common era; common era

think, feel, and especially in the way we behave. And it is done *to* us, not *by* us (as opposed to self-help methods).

You will get the most from this material when you actively participate. Remembering these reflections will help:

What did I read/hear?

What does it mean?

What is my experience?

How does it apply to me?

Scott Peck opens his book *The Road Less Traveled* with the comment: "Life is difficult." The Buddhist first Noble Truth (and much of Judaism) is "Life is suffering." The Christian motif is "pick up your cross and follow me."

Life is not easy. Most definitely the spiritual life is not easy. It is a path that requires "authentic suffering" (Dr. Garrett, Betty Ford Medical Center). Although pain is inevitable—an intrinsic part of the human condition—suffering is optional. Suffering comes not from life's constant changing, but from our resistance to the change.

We live in a culture whose mantra is to "feel good" in all areas of our personal life at all times. We are trained to be "feel good" junkies. Our spiritual aspirations are soaked in this cultural influence.

The reality is that spirituality is not a call to personal comfort, personal peace, or personal happiness. Spirituality is a call to personal *freedom*. Spirituality is an invitation to consciousness, as you answer:

> *Who am I?*
>
> *Why am I?*
>
> *How do I achieve my purpose?*

It is a journey to know your story, your real story—not the myth you've created. It is a path up the mountain to get a bigger perspective—to see how *your* story fits into *our* story, and to become acquainted with *the* story.

Once we've discovered how to answer these questions and develop this perspective, we identify benchmarks for traveling this path with grace, dignity, and a sense of fulfillment.

We are brought to a place of seeing, knowing, and responding. Union is our existence (we are One); communion is our essence (we are relationship). We are invited to recognize ourselves as beings born of Love who find our meaning in being loving.

Then we can realize in our daily lives a sense of ease and comfort, an internal peace, an overwhelming value, and an overriding state of happiness. We experience the results of ecstasy—standing outside of our self.

> Our awareness and enjoyment of personal well-being are by-products of living authentically.

◈

This process is open to all Twelve-Step fellowships (AA, Alanon, NA, CA, MA, SA, GA, OA, FA, EA, etc.) and to all individuals who aren't in any Twelve-Step fellowship but are also on a path seeking a spiritual way of life. The Big Book of Alcoholics Anonymous* supports this openness: "... we are sure that our way of living has its advantages for all." (*Alcoholics Anonymous* "Big Book" page xiii—Foreword to the First Edition)

This book is intended to help *all* individuals find a better way of life through enlightenment, transcendence, and a personal relationship with Divinity. It is especially written for those who are sick and tired of being sick and tired, and who don't know what they want but are very sure they don't want what they have.

Buckle up—this is a challenging and exhilarating ride!

Alcoholics Anonymous, published by AA World Services, New York, which its members call "The Big Book" will be referenced as "BB" throughout the remainder of this text.

Definitions

Spiritual Awakening: The Process

A slow change in the way we think, feel, and behave that is done to us, not by us.

Spirituality: The Result

Living the realization that there is only one Reality and I am (and you are) a manifestation of It. This is realization of Oneness, a place of non-duality, a space of authentic Union and Communion. Direct consciousness, awareness of the presence of God.

Enlightenment: The Process—Wisdom

"Simple but not easy. A price has to be paid. It means the destruction of self-centeredness. I must turn (be turned) in all things to the Father of Light who presides over us all." (BB page 14) This is usually a slow process of an improvement in awareness, an increase in consciousness, a movement toward spiritual awakening.

Loving Service: The Path—Compassion

The true self is that original self that God willed into being. Coming from Love, living in Love, having a destiny of conscious union with Love, the self is most real, most authentic, most true, and is experienced most fully when that self is loving!

Oxford Group Origins

Sam Shoemaker, an Episcopal priest, was the leader of the Oxford Group in the 1930s. The Oxford Group, originated by Frank Buchman, a Lutheran minister, was an attempt to recreate first century Christianity. It developed six steps to spiritual conversion:

1. Complete deflation

2. Dependence on and guidance from God

3. Moral inventory

4. Confession

5. Restitution

6. Continued work with others

These are the steps taken by:

- Roland Hazard after his meeting with Dr. Carl Jung;

- Ebby Thacher after being brought to the Oxford Group by Roland;

- Bill Wilson after his introduction to the Oxford Group by Ebby;

- Bob Smith after his intervention by Bill.

Bill and Dr. Bob - cofounders of AA - continued their active membership in the Oxford Group after they got sober.

Bill and the New York alcoholics stopped going to Oxford Group meetings sometime in 1937; Dr. Bob and the Akron/Cleveland alcoholics separated from the Oxford Group when the Alcoholics Anonymous book was published in April 1939.

This poem by Sam Shoemaker captures the spirit of sponsorship – a sincere desire to be helpful to others who suffer. Our job is to help them to and through the doorway of a spiritual awakening. My prayer is that this book serves this purpose.

I Stand By the Door

I stand by the door.
I neither go too far in, nor stay too far out,
The door is the most important door in the world—
It is the door through which men walk when they find God.
There's no use my going way inside, and staying there,
When so many are still outside and they, as much as I,
Crave to know where the door is.
And all that so many ever find
Is only the wall where a door ought to be.
They creep along the wall like blind men,
With outstretched, groping hands.
Feeling for a door, knowing there must be a door,
Yet they never find it ...
So I stand by the door.

The most tremendous thing in the world
Is for men to find that door—the door to God.
The most important thing any man can do

Is to take hold of one of those blind, groping hands,
And put it on the latch—the latch that only clicks
And opens to the man's own touch.
Men die outside that door, as starving beggars die
On cold nights in cruel cities in the dead of winter—
Die for want of what is within their grasp.
They live, on the other side of it—
live because they have not found it.
Nothing else matters compared to helping them find it,
And open it, and walk in, and find Him ...
So I stand by the door.
Go in, great saints, go all the way in—
Go way down into the cavernous cellars,
And way up into the spacious attics—
It is a vast, roomy house, this house where God is.
Go into the deepest of hidden casements,
Of withdrawal, of silence, of sainthood.
Some must inhabit those inner rooms,
And know the depths and heights of God,
And call outside to the rest of us how wonderful it is.
Sometimes I take a deeper look in,
Sometimes venture in a little farther;
But my place seems closer to the opening ...
So I stand by the door.

There is another reason why I stand there.
Some people get part way in and become afraid
Lest God and the very zeal of His house devour them;
For God is so very great, and asks all of us.
And these people feel a cosmic claustrophobia,
And want to get out. "Let me out!" they cry.
And the people way inside only terrify them more.
Somebody must be by the door to tell them that they are spoiled
For the old life, they have seen too much:
Once taste God, and nothing but God will do any more.

Somebody must be watching for the frightened
Who seek to sneak out just where they came in,
To tell them how much better it is inside.

The people too far in do not see how near these are
To leaving—preoccupied with the wonder of it all.
Somebody must watch for those who have entered the door,
But would like to run away. So for them, too,
I stand by the door.
I admire the people who go way in.
But I wish they would not forget how it was
Before they got in. Then they would be able to help
The people who have not yet even found the door,
Or the people who want to run away again from God.
You can go in too deeply, and stay in too long,
And forget the people outside the door.
As for me, I shall take my old accustomed place,
Near enough to God to hear Him, and know He is there,
But not so far from men as not to hear them,
And remember they are there, too.
Where? Outside the door—
Thousands of them, millions of them.
But—more important for me—
One of them, two of them, ten of them,
Whose hands I am intended to put on the latch.
So I shall stand by the door and wait
For those who seek it.
"I had rather be a door-keeper ..."
So I stand by the door.

From *An Apologia For My Life*
By Samuel Moor Shoemaker
(written around 1929)

— ASLEEP —

In the Beginning ...

Separation and Brokenness

— ASLEEP —

In the beginning our consciousness is that we are our origin and the center of our universe. Decades later, if we are on an authentic path of human (spiritual) evolution, our consciousness is that we are One with our Origin; Universe is our center.

Union with our Origin is not the initial issue—it is the reality. As (or if) we evolve, union with the self and communion with others are the interim realization. Eventually, union becomes the consciousness (spirituality) and the journey becomes the destination (transformation).

This assumes that we are willing to respond to Grace.

> We are all invited to a cosmic dance of Grace
> and willingness

The evolution is not just to transform, but to transcend—not *by* the self but *through* the self. This is done by a series of decisions and actions. To be changed and to return to our Origin—union through communion.

We listen to the small voice inside and decide accordingly. We have an experience. We learn. We listen again and take an action that produces an experience ... and once more we learn. Then we listen some more, respond some more, experience some more. This cycle, once set in motion, can only be interrupted by:

- Not listening attentively

- Not deciding

- Not responding through action

- Not embracing the experience

- Not incorporating the learning

- Not listening again.

Choice is the key.

> Knowledge is good but not sufficient. Nothing happens until a decision is made and an action is taken.

And then there are always consequences!

If the action is out of harmony with the principles of Universe, the consequences will be disharmony; if the action is in harmony with the principles of Universe, the consequences will be harmony—within and around us.

Our life's task is to become aware of and aligned with our true Origin and our true destination. Our true Origin is a creation of Love; our true destination is to serve the Divine in others, and realize our Oneness.

Purpose

Over the first 30 years of my adult life I have been to countless weekends, workshops, conferences, retreats, classes, etc. Usually they are populated with well-intentioned, smart, educated, and serious seekers. At the end of our time together we all separate more or less informed, inspired, hopeful, and resolved. However, because of a lack of applicable content or specific method, we quickly return to our original state of ineffective attempts to self-transform and manage our lives—unable to evolve as human beings, let alone as spiritual beings.

> I did not know that I did not know. I could not see that I did not see. I spent these years asleep, dreaming that I was awake.

Then, as the result of circumstance, Grace, followed by my willingness and action, I began a journey that led to waking up. This was a slow process—but a powerful process.

I cannot change life as it unfolds around me, but I surely can change my perception of it, my attitude toward what is happening, and my reaction to it.

Today my life flourishes. I still encounter the speed bumps, but I have come to a place of self-knowledge, awareness, guided action, and service that allows me a meaningful experience of personal freedom, continuous excitement, and a real sense of value and authenticity. The purpose of this book is to be a guide that inspires others to transform—not to have my experience, but so to have their *own* experience.

> We're not human beings seeking a spiritual experience, but spiritual beings seeking a human experience.

This spiritual path that I've walked over the last 26 years is the Twelve Steps of Alcoholics Anonymous. The miracle of this method is that it distills (pun intended!) the essence of all major spiritual paths—Hinduism, Judaism, Buddhism, Christianity, Islam. If you review an objective comparison of these five traditions, eliminate the jargon, historical context, cultural inflections, religious dogma/ritual and social requirements, these essential principles would remain:

> 1. Love God with all your mind, with all your heart, and with all your strength.
> 2. Love your neighbor as yourself (or better ... as God Loves you).

The nature of human suffering—dis-ease—is self-centeredness. In other words, to the extent we think we are the center of the Universe, we suffer. This attachment to self must change, but it's hard-wired into our person and our culture.

The premise of the Twelve Steps is that an awakening is necessary. This is defined as a change in the way we think, feel, and act—requiring intervention by a Power other than ourselves.

The intent of this work is to document the steps of my journey of transformation.

> My first book may be helpful: *Twelve-Step Guide to Using the Alcoholics Anonymous Big Book: Personal Transformation:* The *Promise of the Twelve-Step Process.*

Preparation

Having a guide is of paramount importance—he or she is a person to:

- Shine the light of their experience on the path they have walked so that we can walk it and have our own experience

- Be a sounding board for questions and concerns

- Hold us accountable to be thorough and consistent

- Inspire us to continue when the going gets rough or we get distracted with our life.

> All people on a spiritual path will be helped by having a spiritual companion, friend, director, sponsor or guide.

Fortunately, I was led to a man as my guide who'd had a powerful personal transformation and was particularly adept at communicating it. Some people do this or similar work with their sponsor; others with their therapist or spiritual director.

He agreed to guide me through the steps on the condition that once I'd finished, and had the guaranteed spiritual awakening (promise of Step Twelve), I would guide others; I agreed.

Process

The formula for this work includes definite ingredients: *prayer, reading, reflection, writing, and discussion.*

Each assignment has a purpose or theme and reflection questions, such as:

- Why do you want to do this work?

- Why at this time?

- Are you willing to go to any length?

- Where are you being dishonest with yourself or others?

Your answers focus and confirm commitment and keep you on track.

After a period of reflection, write out your answers and share them with your guide. Meet regularly to review and discuss your work. The key is to have a personal experience with the material.

My guide made it very clear in words, attitude, and behavior that he was a lantern shining on the path he had walked so that I could also walk it. He was a lantern, not the light. I was to have my own experience—not his. He would show me the path, and walk with me, but I had to do the walking and the work.

The ingredients are described below, as I experienced them:

▪ *Prayer*

Each of us comes to this work with a personal history—knowledge, values, beliefs, and experiences. To the extent that we hold onto these, we are chained to the wall and cannot receive new knowledge, revised values, expanded/different beliefs, or new experiences.

> Einstein said: "The consciousness that created the problem cannot be the consciousness that solves the problem." We need a new approach, a new consciousness, an open mind and heart, a willingness to explore new dimensions.

My guide suggested that I could not bring this about through my own desire or power, but needed the Spirit of the Universe (whatever that means to me) to intervene. He asked me to create a "set aside" prayer. My prayer became:

"Spirit of the Universe, please set aside my ideas and beliefs about myself, You, my brokenness, and the spiritual path of healing so that I am brought to an experience of truth in each of these areas."

I prayed this prayer each morning and anytime I sat down to do this work.

No matter what your history, a prayer like this will help unblock you.

(Note: this is not a "throw away" prayer. Some of our past is productive and constructive. We're just not sure which components are useful and which contain impediments.)

▪ *Reading*

I read two books: *Alcoholics Anonymous* ("Big Book," or BB) and T*he Twelve Steps and Twelve Traditions* ("12 & 12")—both published by AA's World Services, Inc., New York, New York. Specific instructions are in the BB; the 12 & 12 is a commentary by Bill Wilson, AA's co-founder, on his step experience during the first 15 years of his recovery. My guide instructed me to read with intent, using a highlighter to mark words, phrases, sentences, or paragraphs that spoke to me, especially related to that assignment's theme. In addition, I was to make liberal margin notes, underline phrases of special significance, and look up words as necessary to understand the author's intent.

This interactive process allowed the meaning to seep out of the page and into my being—precipitating a new connection, a new understanding, a new experience.

I used a 3x5 card as a bookmark, with four questions to review before I began each reading assignment:

1. What does it say?

2. What does it mean?

3. Is this my experience?

4. How does it apply to my life?

Material that I'd read several times before began to make sense for the first time, and I made connections that helped me see deeper into myself, my condition, and my experience.

▪ *Reflection*

This is not an intellectual or emotional exercise— although the mind and feelings are, and should be, involved. It is a spiritual exercise. We need to bring our actual experience to the process to make it real, to make it ours, to own it. It is not another academic exercise to improve knowledge; it is a practical experience to improve life.

An effective spiritual guide will not give us answers—even though they have answers and would like to help. They know this would be a disservice to the seeker. Your guide will help you ask questions and let the tension of an unanswered question create the energy and space for a response that has personal significance—depth and weight.

• *Writing*

Most assignments included some writing: answers to the questions above, reactions to some part of the reading, or just spontaneous writing to connect the deepest part of our knowing with our consciousness.

My guide pointed out that there are several symbols for the various sources of knowing—the head (information), the heart (intuition), and the gut (instinct). The last two are not easily available to us but can be accessed through writing. Also, when it's in writing we can't easily deny it, rationalize it, or minimize it. It is a very revealing technique.

> Writing wrings the vagueness out of our knowing and makes it concrete.

• *Discussion*

Once the assignment was completed, my guide and I got together to review the work. We looked at each page of the reading and he commented on the words, phrases, and sentences that were meaningful to him. Then I did likewise. We discussed our perceptions, reactions, feelings about our experience. He made it very clear that this was not a test, nor a competition. I did not have to see what he saw. I did not have to have any particular experience—just my own. My guide gave me the dignity of having my own experience. He met me where I was; not where he was.

> We can only see what we can see. We can only see it when we see it—and not a moment sooner.

When we had gleaned what that page had to offer, we went on to the next, then the next, etc., until we had re-viewed the material of each assignment.

Then I read to him any writing that was part of the assignment and he gave me the next assignment.

This process will take its own course. For me, the first time (1988) took 11 months, the second (1991) six months, and the third (1994) two years. Each time I chose a new guide; each time I had a different intention for doing the work; each time there was a deepening and broadening of my consciousness. I know this only in retrospect.

> We rarely know what's happening to us when it's happening.

Only when I look at my path—where and how I'm walking, the impact on those in my life, my reaction to my life—do I sense the effectiveness of this transformation. Richard Rohr says it's only when we look back over our shoulder that our path straightens out.

It's gradual and subtle—but it's powerful. And you'll want more. This thirst can be quenched only by drinking at the Font of Life. By standing outside our false self we are brought to union with our true self.

> "The hole in us is in the shape of God."
>
> –Blaise Pascal

— AWAKENING —

Seeking Healing ...

Instruction and Action

As we begin our journey into and through the Twelve Steps, let's consider the perspectives of the co-founders of Alcoholics Anonymous in a 1948 article "On the Twelve Steps"— published in A.A.'s Grapevine magazine:

Bill Wilson:

"It is gratifying to feel that one belongs to and has a definite personal part in the work of a growing and spiritually prospering organization for the release of the alcoholics of mankind from a deadly enslavement. For me, there is a double gratification in the realization that, more than 13 years ago, an all-wise Providence, whose ways must always be mysterious to our limited understanding, brought me to "see my duty clear" and to contribute in decent humility, as have so many others, my part in guiding the first trembling steps of the then-infant organization, Alcoholics Anonymous.

It is fitting at this time to indulge in some retrospect regarding certain fundamentals. Much has been written; much has been said about the Twelve Steps of AA. These tenets of our faith and practice were not worked out overnight and then presented to our members as an opportunist creed. Born of our early trials and many tribulations, they were and are the result of humble and sincere desire, sought in personal prayer, for divine guidance.

Yet there are no shibboleths in AA. We are not bound by theological doctrines. None of us may be excommunicated and cast into outer darkness. For we are many minds in our organization, and an AA Decalogue in the language of "Thou shalt not" would gall us indeed."

Dr. Bob Smith:

"As finally expressed and offered, they (the Twelve Steps) are simple in language, plain in meaning. They are also workable by any person having a sincere desire to obtain and keep sobriety. The results are the proof. Their simplicity and workability are such that no special interpretations, and certainly no reservations, have ever been necessary. And it has become increasingly clear that the degree of harmonious living which we achieve is in direct ratio to our earnest attempt to follow them literally under divine guidance to the best of our ability."

1

Step One

"We admitted we were powerless over alcohol—that our lives had become unmanageable."

Prayer

God, please set aside everything I know about myself,
my brokenness, the spiritual path, and You, God,
for an open mind and a new experience of myself,
my brokenness, the spiritual path, and especially You, God.

Some readers may choose to replace the word alcohol with 'brokenness.'

Chapter One

Powerless: Name Our Sickness/Brokenness

Bill Wilson said the purpose of all the steps, but especially Step One, is "deflation of the ego at depth." Step One is the foundation of the spiritual structure (arch) that is to be built. We must look at our own actual experience of drinking and living (alcohol—unmanageability) to come to a deep realization of our personal powerlessness—a sense of doom, hopelessness, helplessness.

"Ego" here is not the healthy self-esteem that psychology/psychiatry tries to rehabilitate from the damages created by family dysfunctions or self-destructive behaviors. It is the persona (mask) built over years by our survival efforts—our shadow self (Jung), our false self (Merton/Keating). This is the "ego" that must be deflated. This is the "ego" that must be dismantled. This is the "ego" that must die.

This is not only a head exercise, but a more important one of heart and gut. We need to ask a question (or have it asked) and let it create tension that opens us up to new information, take action, have a new experience—then allow the cycle to repeat.

My full experience of Step One developed over a 10-year period. When I first came into AA (1984) it was the drama that suggested I was an alcoholic: blackouts, jails, car wrecks, etc. Then when I did the steps the first time from the Big Book with a guide (1988), I saw that my body was different—it does not process alcohol successfully. Next (1991) I saw that my mind was different—it does not process reality successfully. It is defective: subject to obsession and delusion. Next (1994), I saw that, despite all my best efforts, I had not changed my behavior successfully; my will is defective. By its very nature, it always wills self = self-centered.

It struck me that the original logo of AA contains a triangle that represents a three-part solution:

Perhaps that's to address a three-fold problem: body, mind, and will. Our body can be detoxed in meetings through fellowship*—held together by the Twelve Traditions (Unity). Our mind can be detoxed through application of the Twelve Steps (Recovery). Our will can be detoxed through the Twelve Concepts (Service).

---

*The Big Book consistently suggests that hospitalization and/or professional treatment may be needed at the beginning of the recovery process.

This model of a three-part problem and a three-part solution is confirmed in the BB page 64: "From it (resentment) stem all forms of spiritual disease for we have been not only mentally and physically ill, we have been spiritually sick. When the spiritual malady is overcome, we straighten out mentally and physically." (See Appendix B for a diagram of the historical contributions of Religion, Psychology, and Medicine to the development of Alcoholics Anonymous.)

Step One has two parts. The first deals with alcohol: "We admitted we were powerless over alcohol ..." (BB page 59).

1. Alcohol

This is about the liquid substance. This half of Step One itself has two parts:

  a. when it's in us   BODY

  b. when it's not in us MIND

The second half of Step One has nothing to do with alcohol: "—that our lives had become unmanageable." (BB page 59)

2. Unmanageability   WILL

This has to do with our life, our actions, our attitudes, our efforts, our results.

Readers who are not alcoholic may want to substitute their particular brokenness for the word "alcohol":

Addictions
      Drugs (illegal and prescribed)
      Food (sugar and caffeine)
      Nicotine
      Gambling
      Spending/debting
      Sex
      Isolation/self-reliance
      Low self-esteem
      Depression (non-clinical)
      Self-pity

Compulsions
      Thinking
      Relationships
      Control
      Exercise
      Anger/depression/fear
      Helping/service
      Work
      Religion
      God
      Etc., etc., etc.

1. The Problem of the **Body**

My assignment was to read the Big Book beginning with the face page, all the Roman numerals, pages 1–8 and 17 through to the top of 23 (skipping pages 9–16 since they describe Bill's experience of the solution). I was to pay particular attention to the Doctor's Opinion (BB pgs xxv-xxxii). I was to approach this material from the point of view of my physical body and my actual drinking experiences. What happened when I drank? Did I drink more than I wanted to? Did it happen more than once ... more than 10 times ... all the time?

I was to identify at least three specific experiences when I drank more than I intended or wanted to. Here are some examples:

- A few days before Christmas 1980 a business associate asked me to lunch. I agreed with the stipulation that I had only one hour and had to get back to a project at work. We ordered a drink and had lunch. We were finished in 45 minutes and my colleague suggested, since we still had 15 minutes, we have an after-lunch Christmas drink. We had many, stayed there till 5, and then went to a saloon that we closed at midnight. I drove home in a blackout.

- On another occasion, a vendor invited me to lunch to celebrate a mutual sale we had accomplished. We began drinking wine with the meal. We left there at 6 p.m. and went to a saloon. When I left there at 9 p.m., I was arrested for drunk driving and spent the night in jail.

- Regularly I would call home from work confirming that I would be there for our family dinner (which was really important to both my wife and me). Then I'd stop at the bar for "one for the road" and would not come home until midnight or later.

Usually I was in a blackout and didn't remember driving home.

There were literally hundreds of these incidents over 30 years.

The Doctor's Opinion speculates that alcoholics may have an allergy—an abnormal physical reaction to alcohol—which most people don't have. Once we put alcohol into our body, it reacts in a way that demands more alcohol. Dr. Silkworth calls this the "phenomenon of craving." Our very cells demand to be satisfied beyond our ability to control it. Medical science has begun to confirm that alcoholics do not process alcohol like normal people. It has something to do with our genetic make-up. Somewhere in this metabolic process our liver converts alcohol into a chemical (acetone) that sets up a physical craving that must be satisfied with more alcohol; and the more we drink, the thirstier we get. Instead of quenching our thirst, alcohol creates an overwhelming thirst and we are compelled to drink beyond rational consumption. It is like pouring gasoline on fire—it doesn't extinguish it, but makes it more ferocious.

I believe there are two different kinds of alcoholics: chronic and periodic. The chronic needs to drink just about every day, and each time they drink to excess. The periodic can have a single drink one day with no need to continue, yet the next day they will have one, then another, and will get drunk—without intending to. And the periodic can go days and even weeks without a drink or even thinking about a drink; this intermittence masks the problem.

Chronic or periodic, once an alcoholic takes any alcohol whatever into their body the phenomenon of craving is triggered and we will eventually drink more than we wanted to—usually to excess with all its attendant consequences:

- Blackouts
- Drunk driving arrests
- Car wrecks
- Physical abuse
- Verbal arguments
- Lost jobs
- Divorce
- Financial difficulties
- Medical problems (ulcers, cirrhosis, heart attack, etc.)
- Depression
- Etc., etc., etc.

These consequences, which happen to all alcoholics, are not the issue—but they may serve as the wake-up call. They are the drama, not the cause; the symptoms, not the disease.

The issue is the compulsive drinking. The explanation is the presence of a physical allergy that results in the phenomenon of craving *after* we ingest alcohol.

It's really not our fault! We are built like that. Our bodies are different.

Once I put alcohol in my body, I could not stop.

I AM POWERLESS!

The real questions are:

- Why don't we see it?

- What prevents us from awareness of our repeated behavior and the consequences?

- Why don't we just stop and stay stopped—given all the wreckage and pain to ourselves and others?

- Why doesn't the abstinence experienced in jails, hospitals, asylums, recovery homes, alcohol programs, etc. turn out 100% recovery?

- Why do we relapse?

The answer is that we have a problem of the *mind.*

2. The Problem of the **Mind**

What makes us specifically human? Not that we have a body—rocks have physical materiality. Not that we grow—flowers blossom. Not that we move from place to place—animals do that. But no other being has the ability to know and to know that they know. No other sentient being has free will—the ability to make a decision to take action.

> This first component of being human (mind) is discussed here; the second (will) is discussed in the next section.

We think, reflect, have consciousness of our selves as knowing. The "mind" is not an organ. It is the symbol for that in us which allows us to know (not just the brain that generates cognitive thinking). The "heart" is the symbol for that which produces intuition. The "gut" is the symbol for our instincts. The combination of head, heart, and gut is the source in us for knowing. Not a body part, but a faculty, a facility, an ability.

And yet, alcoholics continue to repeat behavior expecting different results, not learning from our experiences. We do not or cannot connect the dots.

Why is that? Pages 23 to 43 in the BB suggest that we have a defective mind—inherently flawed and suffering from an obsession. One idea enters our consciousness and dominates it in such a way that all other ideas are shoved aside. We are possessed by it. The obsession becomes the only reality.

It further suggests that we suffer from illusion and delusion. Illusion is the misperception that something outside us is real, like a mirage. Delusion is the misperception that something inside us is real, such as our idea of how the world should be, our idea of "who I am"—a story we've made up about reality that has little basis in fact but which we believe and we live our life accordingly. The BB says "... they cannot after a time differentiate the true from the false." (page xxvi)

Once again I was asked to read the BB assignment with a focus: what was my experience of controlling or quitting drinking? After a period of intentional abstinence, what was I feeling or thinking just before I began drinking? Was I even aware/conscious of beginning again?

Examples:

- I had a drunk driving arrest in 1968. In those days it resulted in a ticket. I paid the fine. I had another in 1969; another ticket and payment. No thought whatever of a problem. I was so drunk on another occasion that complete strangers drove me home. I had blackouts two or three times a week. I regularly had problems at work, at home, with finances. I got in a bar fight and had to have multiple stitches in both ears and to the back of my head.

I never looked at these events as a problem. I never saw a pattern. I didn't connect the dots. How could this be, given my background of education and self-reflection!

I left the seminary after studying to be a priest for seven years, got a graduate education in psychology, participated in both individual and group therapy, engaged in transcendental meditation, yoga, trans-personal psychology, men's work, retreats, read a multitude of self-help books, became very health-oriented (ran four miles a day, took vitamins, and quit smoking, red meat, caffeine, dairy products, sugar, white flour, etc.). How could I not see that I was drinking too much and that alcohol was a poison? It had never even occurred to me.

Years later, the hospital (where my wife was an inpatient for her drinking) asked me "what is your autobiography of drinking?" I was shocked ... not that I was alcoholic, but that I had not seen it.

▪   I signed up for a self-help training called Life Springs (1980). They asked us not to drink or use drugs for 90 days. No problem. During this time I felt good, so good that I determined to quit drinking. I even went to a hypnotherapist for help in understanding myself and my drinking and to obtain a method for stopping. During three sessions he regressed me and we eventually discovered that I connected drinking to being an adult (early childhood conditioning); he gave me a post-hypnotic suggestion to decouple this conditioning.

All went well for a time. Then I was hosting a dinner, ordered wine for the event, decided to taste it and have a glass (no thought at all about my previous efforts and recent commitment to abstain). Nothing happened that night. However, looking back at this from the vantage point of being in AA, I see that my drinking changed after that. Instead of a glass of wine at lunch with clients I had vodka on the rocks (believing that you can't smell it). After work, rather than scotch and soda, I ordered double scotch on the rocks. My drinking disease had progressed during the time I wasn't drinking.

I was really trying to identify the problem, going to good professionals, paying lots of money, spending a considerable amount of time. Why couldn't I see all this?

▪ As part of my second time (1991) working the steps from the BB with a guide, I was asked why I drank, when I drank, when I quit or tried to control my drinking, and what I was thinking each time I began again.

I remembered that during the last five years of our drinking, my wife and I made a decision to not drink Sunday through Thursday. We'd save our drinking for weekends. We were vaguely aware that alcohol was affecting our lives. On Monday, if I came home and had not been drinking (two big "ifs"), and my wife was drinking, it gave me permission to drink. If she hadn't been drinking, we both circled around waiting for the other to break for the liquor cabinet. Eventually one of us did, which gave the other one permission—and we both had relief. On Tuesday morning we'd once again resolve not to drink until Friday. Tuesday night repeated Monday's scenario. Wednesday repeated the pattern.

I had thought I was making a decision—merely choosing to change my mind. Then I saw the truth: I was not changing my mind; I was compelled to drink beyond my ability to control it.

I did not connect the dots. I was living in that "strange mental blank spot" (BB page 42) where I couldn't see the truth about alcohol.

It was like being color blind. I remembered that in one of my psychology classes, when presented with a color bubble chart and asked to pick out the number, I couldn't do it. My classmate said the number was 7. She placed my finger on the page and drew it where she saw it. I wanted to see it. I believed it was there. I was shown where it was. Yet, because I have a retinal deficiency, my eye couldn't process the color difference.

I got it—I have a mental deficiency which prevents me from processing reality, especially with respect to alcohol. No matter how badly I want to see, no matter how painful the consequences, no matter how clearly the information is presented to me by credible people—I cannot see. And I cannot see that I cannot see!

People talk about denial. They speak the word in a sentence that sounds like an accusation, a judgment: "You are in denial!" Based on my experience with the mental obsession, I had no consciousness, no awareness. Denial was indeed the reality, but not a decision. I had no clue. Life was happening, behavior was manifesting, and I was not connecting the dots. It was not willful—nobody would intentionally create the chaos that's epidemic in an alcoholic's life. There is something wrong with our ability to perceive reality. A friend of mine calls it "reality recognition disorder."

I believed a lie thinking it to be the truth. I lived in a delusion, thinking and really believing it was reality.

> In the same way that our body cannot successfully process alcohol, our mind cannot successfully process reality, especially about alcohol.

Like the bodily affliction, the mental obsession is not our fault. We are built that way. Our minds are different. *I don't know that I don't know. I can't see that I can't see. I am not making a decision; I am being driven by a compulsion. I cannot stay stopped. I will inevitably be once again possessed by the obsession and driven by the delusion—unaware of the lie and its consequences.*

> The mental obsession takes possession of me without my consciousness and without my permission.

I AM POWERLESS!

3. The Problem of the **Will**

Once alcohol has been removed (we are no longer drinking or thinking about drinking) why are most of us "restless, irritable, and discontented?" (BB page xxviii) Why are the events and situations in our life so unmanageable? Why can't we exercise more self-discipline? Why can't we experience more control?

The second component that makes us human is our ability to make decisions. In contrast, an animal can know (process information) and take action. But it cannot stand outside itself, know that it knows, and make a free decision to take action. It's driven by a series of neuron synapse firings and conditioned or instinctual chemical reactions. The human, indeed, has some conditioned or instinctual behaviors. However, when we're acting from our humanness—as conscious beings—we can make specific, free decisions—to read a book, move to California, establish a significant relationship, pursue a particular career, go on a diet (or not!), etc. We call this ability "will."

At the beginning of BB Chapter 4 is a recap of Step One's first half (deficiency of my body; deficiency of my mind). Then there is a transition ... "we could **will** these things with all our might, but the needed power (will?) wasn't there. Our human resources (body and mind?) as marshaled by the *will* were not sufficient. They failed utterly." (BB page 45, emphasis added.)

At nine years of sobriety, I was asked to read the second paragraph on BB page 52, and was instructed to change it slightly to use the personal pronoun and the present tense, then write about my current experience:

I am having trouble with personal relationships.

Yes, I was 27 years married and very unhappy.

I can't control my emotional natures.

Yes, I had mood swings that just seemed to develop without cause.

I am a prey to (devoured by) **misery and depression.**

Yes, I spent a lot of time in self-pity and complaining about my life (and my wife).

I can't make a living.

I had a good career, made lots of money, and liked my work. How did this apply? In prayer the intuitive thought followed the question: I couldn't make a living *that really satisfied me.* There was never enough money, power, prestige, praise, etc.

I am full of fear.

Yes, I was terribly anxious in social situations, always concerned that I'll not get what I want, or I'll lose what I have; that I'll be criticized and/or not measure up.

I am unhappy.

Yes. If only I'd had better parents, more money, better education, more beautiful wife, more competent bosses, etc.

I can't seem to be of real help to other people.

> Yes. And I didn't really care about people or want to be helpful. I wanted the reputation of being helpful but didn't want the inconvenience that went with it.

This paragraph concludes using the word "bedevilments." I looked it up. It means "to be controlled as if by devils." Bill Wilson, in the 12 & 12, speculates that we have a cancer of the soul, a soul sickness, a spiritual malady.

> The predecessor to Alcoholics Anonymous, The Oxford Group, called their six-step process "soul surgery."

My experience was this. At nine years sober, having done the steps from the BB twice (1988 and 1991), with powerful spiritual awakenings each time, I was still plagued with the bedevilments. In 1988, when reviewing my specific drinking history, I experienced the powerlessness of an inherently deficient body—physical allergy producing the phenomenon of craving. In 1991, when reviewing my history of controlling or stopping my drinking, I experienced the powerlessness of an inherently deficient mind—mental obsession producing the strange mental blank spot and the inevitable insanity (unhealthy thinking) of picking up a drink with little or no thought of my past history or probable future consequences (delusion).

Three years later (1994), as the result of using the set-aside prayer and receiving instructions on the new approach to the "bedevilment" paragraph, I began to experience the real source of the trouble. The BB is clear that "... liquor was but a symptom" (BB page 64) and that "bottles are only a symbol." (BB page 103) I was confronted with the true meaning of "unmanageability" and a new dimension of powerlessness.

BB page 60 confirms "the first requirement is that we be convinced that any life run on *self-will* can hardly be a success." BB page 62 confirms the nature of the malady: "Selfishness—self-centeredness!" "... the root of our troubles." It's below the ground—the root, unseen by the naked eye or even the conscious mind. It is the source that manifests in "... fear, self-delusion, self-seeking, and self-pity." "... The alcoholic is an extreme example of *self-will* run riot ..." (BB page 62).

We must be rid of this selfishness—and we cannot accomplish this with our own efforts. Not only can we not get rid of it—we can't even *reduce* self-centeredness much by wishing or trying with our own power. The implication: we are powerless; our will is inherently flawed, deficient, broken. We always choose ourselves—no matter what kind of façade we put on our actions.

But we're under the delusion that if we only manage it better next time, the results will be different. And we try. And we repeat the insanity, believing it will be different with more effort.

Perhaps this human condition is not limited to alcoholics. The BB suggests that alcoholics are an "extreme example." Perhaps this flaw, this deficiency, this crack in our will is the origin of human difficulties, the origin of missing the mark (the origin of sin?). And we experience the folly of repeated actions with identical results. We believe we can know more. We believe we can try harder. But the results still fall far short of expectations, needs, and desires. We cannot rely on ourselves. We repeat the cycle of failure.

I AM POWERLESS!

◈

> "When the spiritual malady is overcome, we straighten out mentally and physically."
>
> (BB page 64)

The foundation of this spiritual process is having a *personal experience* of powerlessness:

- *My body is inherently flawed—of its very nature. It is biochemically different. It cannot successfully process alcohol.*

  I am powerless!

- *My mind (the aggregate of all the ways of knowing) is inherently flawed—of its very nature. My mind is really different from normal people's minds. I cannot successfully process reality not only when it comes to alcohol, but in other situations as well. I cannot seem to learn from my experiences. I do not think of the consequences. I do not connect the dots.*

  I am powerless!

- *My will (the faculty in me that makes decisions) is inherently flawed—of its very nature. It will always choose me even though I want to think my motives are of the highest ideal. Underneath, it's all about me and my will is powerless to make it otherwise. I cannot fix my broken will with my broken will. The decision or action will always come from my brokenness. And I can't see that I can't see. And I don't know that I don't know.*

  I am powerless!

Thus inside my skin there is no solution: my body, mind, and will are inherently defective = powerless. I am hopeless, doomed, based on my own experience. The result is an implosion into helplessness. Bill Wilson calls this deflation of the ego at depth. I must concede to my innermost self that I have no power. Based on my own actual experience I find myself in a deep pit of personal powerlessness.

> "At the center of sin is salvation."
>
> –Thomas Keating

I must experience my powerlessness so that it becomes the launching pad of desperation to seek and find Power.

The spiritual masters of all traditions talk about death and re-birth/resurrection as the process of personal transformation or enlightenment. Eckhart Tolle ("Power of Now") suggests we must die before we die, in order to realize there is no death.

The St. Francis prayer concludes that "... we die to awaken ..."

The BB (page 14) suggests we must pay a price ... the destruction of self-centeredness. And that this is accomplished by ... turning to the Father of Light who presides over us all.

If I am to survive (and perhaps thrive), I must find a Power other than myself or any other human source.

Out of the Depths

"Powerlessness feels very uncomfortable, and the more powerless we realize we are, the worse it feels. This is not a "feel-good" step, since the purpose of it is to empty out any residual notion that we actually have any power within to help or heal ourselves. When we are dredging the bottom and realize there's nothing there, we are starting to do this step. We have to become childlike, totally dependent. We have to find an inner lack of strength. We have to be entirely dependent on forces and events that are outside our control. We have nothing to add, nothing to offer. The ground under our feet is not held up by our own power. The walls around us are not held up by our own power. It is like waiting for the executioner to arrive, sitting in solitary confinement. Friendless, no contacts, no favors owed, no hope.

It is lonely, and since we are totally vulnerable we are entirely afraid—fear pours out of our pores. This is reality, a reality that we try to hide. We try to convince ourselves it doesn't apply to us. But that is not true. There is no depth to which we could not sink, no wretchedness that we are not prepared to try.

The world's worst hangover, the hand of an arresting officer, a final tax demand, or the utter scorn of someone we love might trigger it. It may come to us at full force, or it may creep up on us.

It may be a known fear, it may be unknown, but the certainty lies there, deep in the pain, deep in the awareness: we have sunk as deep as it is possible to go. All that can happen is that the waters flow to cover us up, to wash us away, and cleanse the world of our miserable selves."

Steps of Transformation, Father Meletios Webber

Summary

Purpose	Name our sickness/brokenness (actually experience powerlessness)
Instructions	Read and highlight: 1. Body: BB face page–top of page 23 2. Mind: BB pages 23–43 3. Will: BB pages 44–45; 52; 60–62 Step One in the 12 & 12.
Process	Identify specific/actual/personal experiences with: 1. Physical allergy which leads to phenomenon of craving 2. Mental obsession which reveals we cannot see, we do not know, we don't learn from our experiences 3. Spiritual malady which confirms that even today we can't manage our lives; we will always choose self without intervention from outside self.
Experience	**Powerlessness**: We have *no* power to effectively make decisions over: 1. Alcohol - When it's in us (*after* the first drink) - When it's not in us (*before* the first drink) 2. Our selfishness.
Result	Collapse into a sense of hopelessness and doom: a personal experience of powerlessness.
Promise	Deflation of self, resulting in emptiness—the condition of desperation which moves us to seek and be open to a Power other than ourselves.

Reflection Questions

Body
1. What is my experience of addiction? (wow)
2. What happens when I indulge in this addiction? List 3 examples.
3. What is my history of attempts to deal with it? Describe 3 examples.
4. How successful have I been?
5. How honest have I been about it with others or myself—my efforts and my failures?

Mind
1. Have I ever made a resolution or promise to stop a specific behavior or start a specific behavior?
2. What do I think or feel just before I engage in (or not start) that specific behavior *again*? Am I even pre-conscious? Or am I into it before I realize it?
3. How soon do I realize that I am doing (or not doing) it *again*?
4. How does that make me feel?
5. Do I make another/stronger resolution to stop (start)?
6. How well does this work? How successful have I been?
7. How honest have I been with others or myself about it—my efforts and my failures?

Will
1. Am I having trouble with personal relationships?
2. Can I control my emotions?
3. Am I a prey to misery and depression?
4. Do I derive satisfaction from my way of life?
5. Am I or can I be self-supporting?
6. Do I feel useful?
7. Am I full of fear?
8. Am I unhappy?
9. Am I able to be of real help to others? Do I care?
10. How honest have I been with others or myself about these issues—my efforts and my failures (my doubts)?

Meditation

My human resources (body and mind) as marshaled by my will have failed utterly.

Lack of power is my dilemma.

I must find a Power greater than me. But where and how will I find this Power?

By searching fearlessly!

By searching diligently!

By thinking honestly!

This Power is deep down inside of me—and that is the only place this Power can be found. We can tap into this unsuspected inner resource. What prevents me from making this contact—what are the obstacles? What is blocking me from conscious, effective contact with this Power?

Selfishness—self-centeredness! This is the root of my problem. Selfishness, self-centeredness is manifest in resentment, fear, dysfunctional sex, dishonesty, secrets, guilt, and shame.

I am powerless to see the truth, and I am powerless to take the action.

We sit in the presence of Power—humbly asking to be healed, humbly asking to see the truth, humbly asking to take the action.

> "Let the darkness penetrate your heart and claim you; the darkness will thus provide the light for walking the path."
> —Dr. James Finley

2

Step Two

"Came to believe that a Power greater than ourselves could restore us to sanity."

Prayer

I don't know, I can't see, and I don't really trust that which I cannot understand, observe, or experience.

Please open my mind, my eyes, and my heart to be taken to a place I have never known, never seen, and never experienced. Take me to a place that I don't even know exists.

Please bring me to a real decision about You (faith), a deep acceptance of this decision (belief/hope), and the actions that flow from it (trust/love).

Please, Creative Intelligence, show me who You are. Please give me the humility to know You and to trust You. Let me see reality as You see reality and not be misled by my obsessions, illusions and delusions, superstitions, prejudices, and old ideas.

Please, reveal to me what and who You are.

Please help me come from faith through trust to Love.

Chapter Two

Power: Name the Healer

Powerless! That is the conclusion of the process so far. Inside of our skin—body, mind, will—we have no effective power with respect to alcohol or self. We have no choice. The mental obsession condemns us to drink when we don't want to and the phenomena of craving condemns us to continue drinking once we start. And even when we're not drinking or thinking about drinking, life is unmanageable. Our efforts, energy, desire have not delivered the hoped-for results. We are restless, irritable, and discontent. "Our human resources, as marshaled by the will, were not sufficient; they failed utterly." (BB page 45)

Lack of power is the dilemma—we have to find a Power other than ourselves.

The first three times I did the steps (1984, 1988, 1991) I approached Step Two with the beliefs I'd acquired over my life to date—Catholic schools through college including seven years in the seminary. I believed I believed.

In 1994, the man who was going to take me through the BB steps asked me to pray a set-aside prayer. He knew I had lots of information and wonderful previous experiences with the step process. He also knew that as long as I held onto this information and these experiences I would be blocked from new information and a new experience.

He asked that I write out an answer to: "What is my real belief in God?" He made it clear that he didn't want what I thought, knew, had been told, or would like it to be. What did I really *believe*?

He suggested that when asking myself this question, I look at my behavior because how I behave is what I believe. What *I believe* I believe may in fact be a delusion.

As I reflected on this question I acknowledged that the word "God" is only a symbol—western civilization's shorthand for naming that which cannot be named. Other cultures had other names:

- Hinduism—Brahman

- Judaism—Yahweh

- Buddhism—Enlightenment (not a being, but a state of being)

- Christianity—Trinity and Jesus

- Islam—Allah.

All of them attempt to name the ultimate and unnamable Mystery at the foundation of reality.

Chapter 4 of the BB, "We Agnostics," addresses both agnostics and atheists. "Agnostic" comes from the Greek word *gnosis* which means *knowledge*. The prefix *a* is a negative, and means *no*. Therefore, an "agnostic" is a person who says the existence of God is unknowable.

"Atheist" comes from the Greek *theos*, which means God. The prefix *a* again is a negative. An "atheist" believes there is no God.

I don't have to know (everything)

Goal: release religious resentments
"Religion is a bastardization of a [GOD] good idea".

Both agnostics and atheists are correct—in a way. A human's finite mind cannot know what it is we symbolize by the word God: the Infinite, Uncaused Cause—the Source of all that is. And any word we use is totally inadequate.

I was asked to read Chapter 4 from the perspective of doubt. Do I have any *doubt*, any negative reaction to any word or phrase in the reading, any resistance to any of the implied concepts or names for God?

I knew I didn't have any intellectual doubt. I could sit and discuss the history of religion, comparative religions, the theology of the Trinity, etc. But when I looked at how I was living my life, I was startled to discover my agnosticism—I doubted the Power of God in my life. That became obvious when I reviewed my approach to unmanageability through looking at the bedevilments (BB page 52) and the material on self-will (BB pages 60–62). I also had real resistance to a phrase in Bill's story "... I admitted for the first time that of myself I was nothing; that without Him I was lost." (BB page 13).

I was a practical agnostic! I lived my life as if God were irrelevant. It was all about getting information and technique and trying really hard. It was all about *my* power.

"performance"

Obviously the set-aside prayer was beginning to have its way with me. My mind and heart were being opened to a new truth. I saw the lie I lived: "I have the power; I can rely on my efforts, my knowledge, my gifts, my books, my retreats, my classes, my intention, my intelligence, and my willpower to achieve what I want—even to be spiritual and to transform myself."

Looking over my shoulder, at my actual experience, I saw the lie and the truth.

I had not really been touched by all my study of formal religion, formal psychology, the variety of self-help programs of the 60s, 70s, 80s, or even my first four years in AA. I had not changed. I had been relying on my own power. And I saw, at a new level, that I am powerless without the intervention of Grace—the power of God that creates and flows as the Universe. *grace*

Bill W. was put at ease by Ebby Thacher in their first encounter when Ebby said "Bill, choose your own concept of a power greater than yourself." He realized it didn't matter *what* you call It, just that you *do* call upon It!

> The names given to God over the centuries derive from a particular time, need, and culture. Unfortunately, humans get attached to a certain name— as if their truth is *the* truth and the only truth.

The secret to AA is that it's a spirituality where God remains anonymous—without any specific/required name (paraphrase from Father Webber's "Steps of Transformation"). The BB's perspective is that "the Realm of the Spirit is broad, roomy, all inclusive; never exclusive or forbidding to those who earnestly seek." (BB page 46)

It is noteworthy that the BB Step One discussion encompasses 34% of the instructions (considering all pages with Roman numerals and pages 1–164). Bill W. uses an architectural analogy of an "arch through which we passed to freedom" (BB pages 47, 62, and 75) to describe the building process of the first five steps. We assume Step One is the foundation to the spiritual structure that will be built through completion of all Twelve Steps. Bill W. refers to Step Two as the "cornerstone." (BB pages 47 and 56) A cornerstone is the first stone put on the foundation and determines the direction of the entire structure that is to be built (the spiritual arch).

The absolute point of the Step One discussion is that we have no power of decision:

- After not drinking for a time (day, week, month, year, decade), having made a firm decision not to drink, and having one or more really good reasons not to drink (judge, wife, employer, doctor)—with little or no thought at all we drink again.

- Once we start, we cannot stop.

- Our life—before and even after we stop drinking— is an extreme example of self-will run riot. "Selfishness—self-centeredness! That, we think, is the root of our troubles." (BB page 62) As St. Paul says: we do what we don't want to do and we don't do what we want to do. We seem possessed—as if by devils (recall the bedevilment paragraph from BB page 52).

It's almost ironic that after underscoring this point (that we have no power of decision) the BB, preparing us for Step Two in Chapter 4, now asks us to make a decision. "Do I now believe, or am I even willing to believe, that there is a Power greater than myself?" (BB page 47)

At this point the Big Book is very gentle. One does not have to believe—only be willing to believe. It is a decision—an act of the will. Not about alcohol or about self, but *about* God.

Then the Big Book turns up the burner on page 53 by reminding us about our Step One experience "... crushed by a self-imposed crisis ..." that we have no power and we are going to live miserably and then die prematurely. So "... we had to fearlessly face the proposition that either God is everything or else He is nothing. God either is, or He isn't. What was our choice to be?" (BB page 53)

Again—a decision: not about alcohol or about self, but *about* God.

So what is faith? The dictionary says it is a belief which cannot be proven. Upon reflection, I approached this question using the paradigm of the triangle—the human being made up of body, mind, and will.

Is faith a function of the body, the adrenal glands, or feelings and emotion? Whether or not I "feel" God is present is irrelevant. This is a critically important thought. Most people are feel-good junkies ... forever chasing happiness as the goal of life. Especially in prayer, people look for a feeling of elation, of consolation through God's Presence. And when there is no feeling, or worse, when there is an experience of desolation, they conclude God is absent or has abandoned them. Common sense reveals that faith is not a feeling.

Is faith a function of the mind? The mind knows reality as it is presented through the senses or created through the imagination. The mind is about knowledge and certitude. Faith is the acceptance of that for which there is no evidence. Faith is the opposite of knowledge and certitude. Therefore, faith is not a function of the mind.

What's left in the make-up of the human being? *Will* !

> Faith is a decision, a choice,
>
> a function of the *will*.

When we decide to believe in God, we have no concrete evidence, and perhaps no particular feeling about it. Faith— the decision—is very thin, obscure, empty, and dark. No wonder Bill W., along with centuries of philosophers and theologians, exclaims that people of faith have courage. They make a decision without any knowledge, evidence, certainty, or feeling—then live their life as if this decision is based on the truth.

The will decides; that is *faith*.

The mind accepts the decision as reasonable; that is *belief*.

The body then acts accordingly; that is *trust*.

Perhaps this is the underlying dynamic of the three cardinal virtues: FAITH leads to belief which gives us HOPE; belief put into action is trust; a body in action for God and others is LOVE.

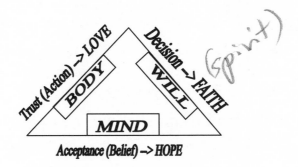

On page 45, the BB asks "where and how were we to find this Power?" Then 10 pages later, on page 55, we receive the answer:

"Sometimes we had to search fearlessly, but He was there. He was as much a fact as we were. We found the Great Reality deep down within us. In the last analysis it is only there that He may be found."

"... think honestly ... search diligently within yourself ..." "With this attitude you cannot fail. The consciousness of your belief is sure to come to you."

Search diligently!

Search fearlessly!

Think honestly!

These describe the attitude necessary for faith and our first conscious contact with God. In sailing, "attitude" is the position of the sail that allows it to catch the wind and power the ship to move forward. Perhaps "searching" and "thinking" are the ingredients for us to catch the breath of God (inspiration: *spiros* = breath), to be empowered.

Our mind is confined, finite, limited—cannot comprehend Infinity. However, our will can reach out in an unlimited openness to embrace and be embraced by the Light.

All life, especially spiritual life, is a dynamic and rhythmic process of ascent, descent, and ascent again.

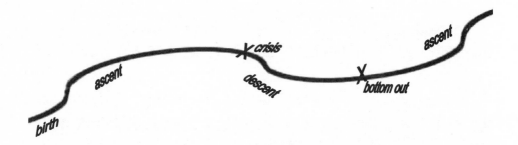

If we're consistent with efforts in life, especially spiritual life, this undulation, this wave-like motion, continues to repeat.

Ken Wilber ("Eye of the Spirit") describes this as a process of attachment, detachment, and transcendence—a spiral process (not linear).

As we progress, the valley experienced later on may be higher than a previous peak, but is nevertheless felt as a valley. However, if we remain faithful to the journey, we show inevitable progress over a lifetime.

Without this undulation, life becomes a flat line.

———————————————————————— = no life.

The AA and Al-Anon logos symbolize two aspects of this Mystery, this Divinity:

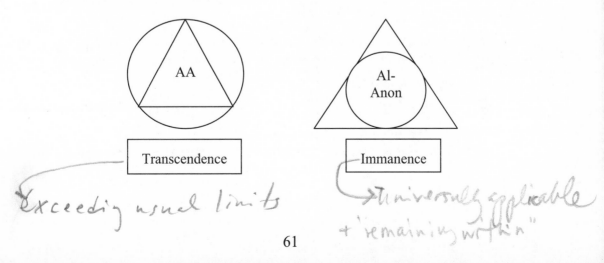

| AA | Al-Anon |
| Transcendence | Immanence |

Exceeding usual limits

→ Universally applicable + "remaining within"

- BB, page 14, "Father of Light who presides over us all."
- BB, page 568, "... we shall forever live in thankful contemplation of Him who presides over us all." (Tradition Twelve)
- BB, page 46, "Spirit of the Universe underlying the totality of things."
- BB, page 55 "We found the Great Reality deep down within us."
- BB, page 567–568, "... tapped an unsuspected inner resource ..."

I remember my second grade teacher explaining God to us in a story about two children who went to the beach for the first time. They brought buckets to play with. When it was time to leave, they wanted to take the ocean with them, so they filled their buckets with water. But they could not take the *whole* ocean with them; their buckets weren't that big. We cannot grasp what is Infinite with our finite mind—it isn't big enough.

Another story: Two little fish were playing in the water. Along came a large fish and, wishing them a good day, exclaimed "Isn't the water grand!?" One of the little fish looked at the other little fish, perplexed, and asked "What's water?"

A few pertinent comments:

- Thomas Merton (Trappist monk) reflected that God is that mystery "whose circumference is nowhere and whose center is everywhere."

- Richard Rohr (Franciscan priest) noted that Genesis (first book in the Hebrew scripture) describes God creating humans in God's image and likeness, and that ever since, humans have made God in their image and likeness. He speculated that "our image of God will change as we do."

- Hildegard of Bingen (mystic from the middle ages) commented that "between God and me there is no between."

- Augustine of Hippo (4th century) wrote that "God is closer to me than I am to myself."

- Meister Eckert (mystic from the 12th century) confirmed that God is "closer to me than the air I breathe."

- Mahatma Gandhi remarked "you will have that God when you become that person."

- Peace Pilgrim (mystic from the 20th century) declared "there is nowhere there is not God."

- Saint Paul (Christian scriptures) pondered "In God I live and move and have my being."

- New Age spirituality and traditional Catholicism (Encyclical, "The Mystical Body of Christ") added "we come from, live in, and evolve toward union with God."

Ask yourself: who do *you* need God to be?

If we have no human power to deal effectively with alcohol or the spiritual malady of self-centeredness, then God needs to be powerful.

If our minds are inherently defective and we can't see that we can't see, and we don't know that, then God needs to be knowing.

With an eye on Step Three (having a relationship with that Power), God needs to be present, accessible, personal, and above all, caring.

Once you make those decisions about who God is for you, you will have taken Step Two. Your cornerstone is in place.

Step Two promises are on BB page 57: "... He has come to all who have honestly sought Him. When we drew near to Him, He disclosed Himself to us!" (The BB was published in 1939, before sensitivity to inclusive gender language. Clearly, God has no gender, but gender-laden words are just another deficiency of language to describe God.)

> "God always sees us; God waits patiently for us to be aware of Him. Being worthy of God's love is like auditioning for a part we already have."
>
> –Cynthia Bourgeault, *"Wisdom of Jesus"*

Dr. Carl Jung, in a 1961 response to a letter from Bill W., suggested that alcoholics are people looking for Spirit and getting distracted by spirits. Dr. Jung suggested that Spirit is the antidote to spirits (see Appendix D for Dr. Jung's letter).

Step Two suggests that we will be restored to sanity. "Insanity" is first used in the BB on page 37 in reference to Jim's story. (We talked about insanity/mental obsession in our discussion of Step One.) BB, page 57, states "Seemingly he could not drink even if he would. God had restored his sanity." That is, God had removed the mental obsession to drink. He now has the ability to think straight.

Look at this statement from the BB. I believe it means he could not drink even if he wanted to. What does it mean to lose the power of choice? We know from our experience that it surely means we cannot *not* drink. But the BB is boldly stating that we cannot drink—if we are under the protection of the Grace of God. We have indeed lost the power of choice: to not drink and also to drink.

This is my experience. On February 20, 1984, alcohol was removed without my request and without my permission. I did not know I was an alcoholic. I did not even know I had a problem with alcohol. I did not make a decision to stop drinking forever. And I certainly did not pray to have the problem removed. I just cooperated with the hospital program's request to stop drinking to support my wife's inpatient recovery program. And with that little bit of willingness to help another person, alcohol was forever removed from my life. It was another four weeks before I experimented with AA, and yet another 3 weeks before I declared I was an alcoholic.

Grace and willingness—a mysterious dance!

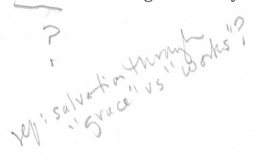

Summary

Purpose Find Power in naming the Healer

Instructions Read and highlight:

1. BB pages 44–57

2. BB Appendix II

3. Bill's story, BB pages 9–16

4. Step Two in the 12 & 12.

Process Identify:

1. Your current actual belief about God

2. Any doubt and resistance to this belief

3. Qualities you need God to have.

Experience Atheism (disbelief) and agnosticism (doubt)

1. Inability to adequately comprehend God

2. The need to make a decision = FAITH

Result A decision to name the Power greater than yourself in a way that works for you.

Promise Certain conscious contact.

Reflection Questions

1. Am I convinced, from my personal experience, of my desperate need for a Power other than myself?

2. Do I have resistance to concepts of God or Higher Power based on old ideas from my family or formal religion?

3. Do I have any doubt or reservations about the existence and availability of a Higher Power?

4. What is my current *belief* about God (not thought, or feeling, or desire)?

5. How does my current belief influence the way I behave (or does it)?   ○ *behaving your way into better thinking + feeling*

6. Am I willing to make a decision about God or a Higher Power without evidence and without feeling attached to it?   *fleeting experiences*

7. What qualities/attributes do I need God to have?

8. How big is God? How powerful is my Higher Power? How caring is my Creator? Does my Higher Power know my name and needs?

Meditation

We sit acknowledging our powerlessness to ...

- Heal our brokenness

- Fix our spiritual malady

- Mend our defective self-will

- See the truth with our broken minds

- Take the required, consistent action with our defective bodies

- Become really awake and conscious with this defective consciousness that created the chaos of this life.

So we sit humbled, in faith—having decided that:

- There is a Power (Energy, Source, Force, Healer, Creator)

- This Power is:
    - Everything
    - All Knowing
    - All Love
    - All Power
    - All Present
    - All Caring

- This Power knows each of us personally.   (con't)

We prepare to make another decision: to surrender, to turn our will and our life over to the care of this Power. And we humbly ask to be taken to a place of utter surrender without reservation—and for the willingness to be taken.

We sit in prayer trusting that this Power will help us:

- Surrender

- Take the indicated action

- Name the obstacles through inventory

- Pierce the illusions of who we think we are

- Dissolve our delusions so we can see the truth of who we really are.

And we sit in gratitude knowing that our being here is Grace, but also that our being here is a witness to our willingness to respond to Grace.

3

Step Three

"Made a decision to turn our will and our lives over to the care of God as we understood Him."

Prayer

I must choose to be directed by a benevolent Power,
or be condemned to be ruled by the tyranny of self.
God, please give me the courage to choose a relationship
with You.

Chapter Three

Decision: to Have a Relationship With That Power

Our experience with Step One makes it clear we have no personal power of decision: over alcohol or over self-will. And yet as we saw in Step Two, we're asked to make a decision—not about alcohol and not about self—but *about* God.

We did that—naming our own concept of God, in an act of faith—a decision of will. No proof! No feeling! Just a decision.

Now we're being asked to make yet another decision—to have a *relationship with* that Power. This is the "turning point." (BB page 59) On BB page 14, Bill W. says: "Simple, but not easy; a price had to be paid." What's the price? "It meant the destruction of self-centeredness." Not a gentle process! How does that take place? "I must turn in all things to the Father of Light who presides over us all." My personal experience would suggest alternate wording to: "I must *be* turned."

My history and education had given me information and exposure, but not a turning point ... a personal or spiritual change. They did not touch me—the me under the me—the real self. They all fostered the false self, the shadow side. But I did not know that I did not know; and I could not see that I did not see.

BB page 60 asks "What do we do?"; page 62 suggests that we quit playing God—because it doesn't work—and that

74

we *decide to establish a relationship* with God instead; the BB characterizes it as:

- Director—Actor

- Principal—Agent

- Father—Child

- Employer—Employee

- Maker (Creator)—Creature.

I was asked to choose one. The first time through this work I chose Father-Son; the second time, Creator-Creature; the third, Guide/Mentor-Pupil/Apprentice.

People I have guided along this path have been wonderfully creative, selecting: Coach, Teacher, Healer, Lover, Architect, Engineer, Master, etc.

The point is to find a relationship that has personal meaning to you at the time you are doing this work. In prayer, be guided by the Spirit to select the relationship that will foster your spiritual evolution.

To expand on the BB's architectural analogy of an arch to freedom (Page 75): Step One is the foundation, Step Two the cornerstone, Step Three the keystone. Perhaps Step Four represents the building blocks and so on ... as illustrated below.

Delrie
mary lynn
(Becky) & Nancy?
→ susan?
Sarah (not here
on 1/4)
Harriet
Ruth

3. Relationship		
4. Selfishness		4. Guilt
4. Dishonesty		4. Shame
4. Sex		5. Secrets
4. Fear		6/7. Humility
4. Resentment		8. Harm
2. Power		9. Amends
(I am) 1. Powerless		

the corner stone

willing to

Step Three is a decision (*for* God—a decision to turn (or be turned) ... a surrender of our will and life.

BB reminders for this process include:

... give yourself completely

... decide to go to any length

... remember half measures won't work

... think well before taking this step

... voice it without reservation

... abandon yourself utterly

... be entirely ready

... ask with complete abandon

... take this position sincerely, honestly, and humbly.

What an order!

> Willingness is the key.
>
> But Grace is the power to turn that key.

from HP

Which comes first, God's Grace or my willingness? This is as unanswerable as the chicken vs. the egg.

I took this question into meditation, and I saw: I was taken to a place of willingness and I was willing to be taken.

I was asked to prepare for this step by writing out my own Step Three prayer—not an exercise to improve the suggested prayer in the BB (page 63), but to understand it by attempting to paraphrase it. Thus I was to reflect on the meaning of the words and phrases and to discern the prayer's underlying direction and principles. The BB Step Three prayer is:

"God, I offer myself to Thee—to build with me
and to do with me as Thou wilt.
Relieve me of the bondage of self,
that I may better do Thy will.
Take away my difficulties, that victory over them
may bear witness to those I would help
of Thy Power, Thy Love, and Thy Way of life.
May I do Thy will always!"

This prayer does not have an Amen. Perhaps this indicates it begins a process that concludes with the Step Seven prayer, which does have an Amen. We are moving toward naming the false self (Step Four), shedding on it the light of confession (Step Five), naming the behavior disorders that manifest from this shadow self (Step Six) and, in recognition of our real powerlessness, asking God to intervene and remove or mitigate them as needed (Step Seven). We are restored to our humanity; we are placed in harmony with our true self. Amen.

My guide asked me to center myself, in silence, in the Presence of that Power I had decided *about* in Step Two and be clear about my decision *for* this new relationship. In this meditation period I realized that the suggestions of my guide (holding hands, on our knees, and praying out loud) were not Step Three. *The decision to form a new relationship* was Step Three. The prayer ritual was a public witness to this decision. First I prayed my prayer, then, together we prayed the prayer from the BB.

> Meditation was part of my preparation—
> reflecting on the process, its meaning, and its
> implications

I envisioned a leap from the bridge of reason to the shore of faith. I called up an image of the Greek athlete—ready to leap across the chasm—as a symbol for the decision to establish this new relationship. As I was lost in this meditation, I became aware that I had already been carried across the chasm in the gentle palm of a Loving Hand ... that I had not leaped at all, but was *taken* to the shore.

I was startled at the recognition of this Gift. And I again became acutely aware that the Twelve Steps are not another self-help program, but a process for submitting to a Power greater than ourselves.

This experience confirmed that I am powerless "to turn" and must be willing "to *be* turned ..." and reminded me that willingness itself is a Grace.

This means you have some glimmer of hope

> The willingness to surrender is the surrender.
> The willingness to surrender is the result of
> the invitation of the Spirit of the Universe to be
> surrendered!

The Step Three promises are described on page 63 of the BB: God provides what I need (not want), if I keep close to God and perform God's work well. *vs self-will*

As we became established in this new relationship, we became less and less interested in ourselves, more and more interested in what we can contribute to life.

These promises are a not-so-subtle reference to Steps Eleven and Twelve. If I want to *know* what I need, I should practice Step Eleven; once I have my daily vision of what God wants, then I should *do* it—actualize Step Twelve. The dimmer switch was being turned up slowly, a notch at a time...

time. The lights became brighter; the energy more available, more real, more effective.

More Step Three promises from BB page 63:

As I felt new Power flow in, as I enjoyed peace of mind, as I discovered I could face life successfully, as I became conscious of God's presence, I began to lose my fear of:

- Today—the present
- Tomorrow—the future
- Hereafter—even death itself

I was reborn!

The concluding promise:

Step Three is movement toward *conscious* contact with God. We construct a concept of the relationship, then decide to initiate and recognize an actual connection with this Source of Power.

We are built with an insatiable desire for union with our Source. St. Augustine prayed "my heart longs for You and cannot rest until I rest in You.".

> "We don't have a relationship with God; we are a relationship with God."
>
> – Richard Rohr

Summary

Purpose	Decide on a relationship with God
Instructions	Read and highlight:
	1. BB pages 58–63
	2. Step Three in the 12 & 12.
Process	Identify the relationship you need to have with God.
Experience	Made a decision to have this relationship, which makes it happen.
Result	Begin to act as if it has been established.
Promise	A new relationship that begins the "turning" from self to God.

Reflection Questions

1. Do I really believe that I can have a personal relationship with the God of my understanding?

2. What does it mean to turn my will and life over to the care of God?

3. What would this actually look like on a practical day-to-day basis?

4. Do I trust God?

Meditation

To live in God as fish live in water,

Not always awake to this fact, but totally dependent for survival,

neither clinging nor resisting.

To aspire to a shift in consciousness, even a tiny one.

To know what we think, when we're thinking.

To know what we feel, when we're feeling.

To not resist, but to acknowledge and embrace.

To take actions through deliberate choice.

To be present to the moment and to those who witness that moment.

To entrust dependence in each of these moments and know/trust that we're deeply loved

and totally taken care of.

To surrender and fall backward into the abyss of the underlying Soul of the Universe.

And to know that it's all a Gift.

And to be grateful!

This is our practice.

(con't)

To be patient and compassionate with ourselves and others.

This is also our practice.

To come to consciousness; to be awake; to be aware; to be present to the present moment;
to live in now—not yesterday; not tomorrow.

Moving with the flow. Breathe in. Breathe out.
Aware of and focused only on the sacred now.

This is our practice.

Step Four

"Made a searching and fearless moral inventory of ourselves."

Prayer

Please allow me to know what I see,
not just to see what I know.

Chapter Four

Name Obstacles to This Relationship

So far, I'd conceded powerlessness of self (or anyone else), named my belief in God, and decided to have a special relationship with this Power. My decision had been witnessed through prayer with my sponsor/guide.

Since this Power is deep down inside of us, what is preventing us from an effective relationship with It?

> "Not everything can be solved, but nothing can be solved if it is not first faced."
> –James Baldwin
>
> The BB suggests "fact finding and fact facing."
> (page 64)

An effective image is to visualize yourself as a large channel. Life, Power, Grace is like water flowing through this channel and nourishing you. But it gets blocked with the sludge of perceptions, feelings, reactions—blocking you from the sunlight of the Spirit. It is this impediment that ensures continued deterioration, disintegration, desolation, and darkness.

I wrote my first inventory in my first year of sobriety (1984). I read the BB but did not really understand it. I read *to miss the mark*

· attitudes & actions on a continuum

the 12 & 12's description of instincts gone awry, manifesting in the seven capital "sins": pride, greed, sloth, anger, envy, lust, and gluttony. It describes how we're out of harmony with ourselves and the flow of the Universe. But there are no "how to" instructions. I reviewed the literature and questionnaires developed in various AA meetings. As a result, I got thoroughly confused and ultimately paralyzed. I decided to try the autobiographical approach based on the BB instructions for Step Five—to tell someone *all* your life story. (BB page 73) However, for me, this turned out to be a script of behavior, an acknowledgment of guilt, shame, and secrets. It was the best I could do at the time, but it did not uncover "the exact nature of my wrongs." It talked about behavior, not motives, beliefs, and values. It was good enough for me to stick around AA, but it did not become an instrument of insight and change.

Step 4

Based on that superficial inventory I finished the steps, but they did not touch me. I did not change. I continued to be insensitive, dishonest, grandiose, and narcissistic.

In 1988 I was given a double Grace of inspiration: to re-work the steps, and to ask a man to be my guide. We began looking for the obstacles in me to a relationship with Power.

This process is an inventory: an analytical determination of facts, not a judgment about behavior. We are to look at the underlying motives, the causes and conditions, and to identify our values and beliefs. "We searched out the flaws in our make-up which caused our failure." (BB page 64)

The BB identifies the root of the problem as "Selfishness—self-centeredness!" (page 62)

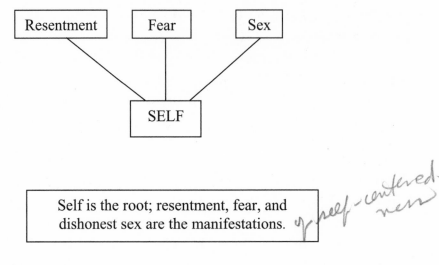

Self is the root; resentment, fear, and dishonest sex are the manifestations. *of self-centered-ness*

These areas represent the primary survival instincts (fight, flight, propagate); there's nothing inherently wrong with these instincts—in fact, our survival depends on their proper use. However, due to our experiences in our family of origin or later with life in general, these reactions can become distorted, dysfunctional, and detrimental. "Our conditioning becomes our straight jacket. Undigested emotional material secretly/unconsciously influencing our feelings, perceptions, and behavior" (Thomas Keating, "Open Mind, Open Heart").

(look up?) I looked at each area …

- **Resentment**

> "*Sentire*" in Latin means to feel; "*re*" means again. Resentment is to feel the anger for an event over and over and over again.

The BB instructs us to list our resentments—the people, institutions, and principles that are the source of these negative feelings (Column One). I was asked to write these down in a head/heart/gut dump (a stream of consciousness purge), then to go through my life in a chronology that made sense for my personal history.

Col.1 I developed a list of 85 names.

Col.2 Once I had a complete list, I was to ask why I had these resentments. (BB page 64) What did these people, institutions, or principles do to me that made me angry (Column Two)?

Then I received instructions for Column Three: how did each event/action affect me? (BB pages 64 and 65)

Now the real analysis began. Dr. Carl Jung refers to our "shadow self." Thomas Merton refers to our "false self." Modern psychology refers to the "persona," the mask we wear without being conscious of the part or the play. Within our attempts at survival and living, we have actually created a story about life, about who people are, how they should act and react, and especially about who we are, how we should be treated, how we should feel and act. Some of the story is correct; some of it isn't. But we live life as if the whole story *all the "shoulds"* is true. When life and the people in it don't act according to our script we get angry.

Column Three begins to pour the acid of reality on this mask and it starts to dissolve.

The BB lists seven variables (pages 64 and 65) that "hurt, threaten, or interfere with" our beliefs. But there are no definitions for these seven words. To properly analyze my resentments, I found it necessary to understand just what these words meant (see worksheet for Column Three in Appendix E 1):

1. Self-esteem—This is not psychology's sense of personal value, but your belief about who you really are—a positive statement such as "I am a person worthy of respect." We're usually not conscious of these underlying beliefs. If you have difficulty seeing self-esteem clearly, go to the second variable (pride) and work backward.

2. Pride—Picture yourself on a stage with the Column One source of resentment; in the audience are your family, friends, coworkers, etc. How do you want other people to see you being treated by the person named in Column One?

3. Ambition—What do you want?

4. Security—What do you need (very different from want)? Why do you need it?

5. Personal relations—How should family, friends, coworkers, etc. see or treat you? Again, use the stage

and audience scenario to come to the truth about how you want to be perceived.

6. Sex relations—Since another section of the Step Four inventory is dedicated to an evaluation of sex conduct (genital), let this variable reveal our beliefs about gender: What is the ideal man? What is the ideal woman?

7. Pocketbook—This concerns your beliefs about money, but if a specific resentment does not have financial implications, perhaps it's about value, emotional price or security, etc.

In the BB, several of these variables have "fear" bracketed next to them (page 65). So you'll note that the Column Three worksheet in the Appendix has a "fear" column on the far right side of each of the seven variables. I found this can reveal some subtle (or not so subtle) truth about beliefs.

NOTE: A more detailed description of this analytical process and the use of the worksheet is contained in my book "Twelve-Step Guide to the Alcoholics Anonymous Big Book."

Column Three analysis is to be applied to each resentment: 1 a, 1 b, 1 c, etc. My guide asked me to do three, then to call him to review them. He indicated this process is not easy since we're not used to thinking about ourselves so analytically. Three times I needed to bring him three examples. Each time he helped me achieve more clarity and insight and finally to break the code. The key is to see "self-esteem" correctly; everything flows from there, which makes perfect sense. Who I believe I am determines how I perceive, feel, and react to my environment. Who I believe I am may be accurate or inaccurate, real or delusional.

I was stunned at what was revealed. Despite all those years of involvement with religion, psychology, therapy, self-help, and AA, I had never seen the arrogance, insensitivity, sense of superiority, entitlement, and uniqueness that dominated my self. Once I had done 10 of these worksheets I began to chuckle at the absurdity and blindness of my self-delusion. It's no wonder I had trouble with other people. Although I had not been conscious of it, I had a world vision that placed me as a king, with the world and its inhabitants here to serve my every need.

And I did not know that I did not know. And I could not see that I did not see.

I experienced a new level of powerlessness—especially with respect to my defective mind and my defective will.

Although I had a profound spiritual awakening as the result of completing this process in 1988, when I did this work again in 1991 my Step Four contained essentially the same 85 resentments. Not only had they not gone away, they hadn't even been mitigated.

In 1991 my new guide directed my attention to BB pages 66 and 67. The first full paragraph asks us to look at "deep" resentments. I was asked to review my 85 and list the "deep" ones separately—those whose tentacles reached down into the marrow of my bones. I had eight: father, wife, two coworkers, and four bosses. The BB indicates we're powerless over these "deep" resentments ("We could not wish them away any more than alcohol!") and suggests:

1. Changing our perception and attitude:

   - Perhaps they are spiritually sick (versus our thinking that they are jerks)

   - Perhaps I'm also spiritually sick (versus better than them)

   - Conclusion: they are human beings struggling to survive just like I am: we're the same.

2. Praying for removal of my resentments.

> We are asking God (the Divine Surgeon/Healer) to perform surgery, to remove this cancerous resentment, to excise it.

I was asked to create a prayer from the last paragraph on BB page 66 and the first full paragraph on BB page 67:

Prayer for Freedom From Resentment

God, (name), like me, is a spiritually sick person. Please help me to show (name) tolerance, compassion and patience.

Please forgive me for being angry and enable me to stop clinging to this resentment. Please remove this

Bless me!
Change me!

resentment and show me how to take a kindly and tolerant view of (*name*). Please show me how I can be helpful to (*name*).

Thy will be done!

Then I was asked to pray this prayer for the removal of each deep resentment. Eight resentments, eight prayers—each day. I began this practice, each day praying the prayer eight times, each time inserting the individual name of the person I deeply resented.

After about two and a half months of consistent prayer, I intuitively knew that one of these resentments had been removed. I scratched that name off the list and continued with seven daily prayers. Then six. Then five. Over the next several weeks these deep resentments evaporated. They were gone.

Now the really good news. When I did this work again in 1994 (with a new guide) and came to the resentment phase, not one of these resentments was there. They had been permanently removed.

indignant
persistent
ill-will

Today, whenever I feel disturbed or annoyed (I very rarely experience resentment), I pray this prayer for its removal. Within a short period (less than 24 hours) the irritation is removed from my consciousness.

Note that this prayer exercise comes *after* the Column Three analysis "when we were finished we considered it carefully." (BB page 65) We need to analyze how these resentments affected us and realize the dysfunctional beliefs that formed our perceptions, feelings, and reactions. We begin to see that our perceptions, feelings, and reactions were based on a lie—a false self—a myth that we conjured up as our story about the world, the people in it, and especially about ourselves.

Next the BB describes a final phase to the analysis of our resentments by suggesting a different perspective. "Putting out of our minds the wrongs others had done, we resolutely looked for our own mistakes." (BB page 67)

For each resentment, we are to ask ourselves:

1. Where had we been selfish?
2. Where had we been dishonest?
3. Where had we been self-seeking?
4. Where had we been frightened?
5. Where were we to blame?

To facilitate this analysis, I created the worksheet in Appendix E 2 (Step Four, Column Four). Let's take a look at how I did the analysis using this worksheet.

Since I am powerless to see the truth, I pray that I can see. And then I try to capture the essence of my self-perception from the Column Three description of self-esteem and specify in Column Four "my role." This is my belief of how I was affected by this event. I am an actor on a stage in the drama of my life. What is the specific role I am playing? Abused child? Misunderstood spouse? Mistreated employee?

The BB suggests that the event may not have even happened, at least as we perceived it ("... fancied or real ..." page 66). Therefore, the worksheet asks if the event actually happened (not the feeling—that certainly is real—but the actual event itself).

And then it lists several questions. The first five are the ones from the BB, but the worksheet includes definitions for the words. Notice that for questions 1 through 5 each definition uses self as the root:

p.302 Worksheet question purpose:

1. Thinking

2. Acting

3. Misrepresenting

4. Losing

5. Blaming

Question 5 is the key. BB page 62 states "So our troubles, we think, are basically of our own making."

The balance of the questions on the worksheet are there to prepare for subsequent step work:

6. & 7.	Harm	in Step Eight the BB indicates we have a list of harms already written out in the inventory process
8.	Fears	preparation for next part of the Step Four inventory
9.	Defects	preparation for Steps Six and Seven.

At the top of the worksheet we were asked to name our role as we perceive it coming out of Column Three. Now this gives us a clue as to our delusion; we really did believe it to be the truth. But we begin to see that it is actually a lie. Once we've answered the nine questions, the worksheet asks us to name our "real role."

Now we can hope to see and name the truth. It's not black and white. Many times others really did behave inappropriately; they really did hurt us. However, some of the times we had a part in the actual event (because of our belief, attitude, or behavior). 100% of the time we are responsible for our perception, feeling, and reaction to the event—not only when it actually happened, but especially now.

As long as we maintain the victim stance we remain emotionally and spiritually sick. As soon as we start taking responsibility for the way we perceive, the way we feel, and the way we behave, we start becoming emotionally and spiritually healthy.

Once again, it's like the dimmer switch that turns the light up one click at a time. Slowly the light becomes brighter. Ever so slowly we begin to see and accept the truth. Glacially slowly the false self—the mask, the persona built over decades—begins to disintegrate and the true you emerges.

- **Fear**

The approach to naming our fears is very straightforward. Make a list. Just like the resentment inventory process, start with a head/heart/gut dump—a stream of consciousness list of fears. Review your life methodically (perhaps buckets of time in chronological order) to identify them.

Additional sources for adding to the fear list include:

- the right hand side of Column Three resentment worksheet

- questions 4 and 8 from the Column Four resentment worksheet.

When the list is finished, take a clean piece of paper and write a prayer at the top, such as "God, please allow me to see the source of my fears." You will recall that both Column Three and Four resentment worksheets requested that we begin the analyses with prayer. Same reason here. We cannot see until we are shown—on our own we're powerless to see the truth.

Take one of the fears and put it on the piece of paper and ask yourself "why do I have it?"; then challenge that answer with "why is that so?"; keep asking "why?" until you come to the underlying cause or begin to go in circles. Here's an example:

> *I have a fear of being honest. Why? Because if I'm honest with you I can no longer manipulate you to see reality or me the way I want you to see it or me. Why is that important? Because when you look at me as I want to be seen, I see reflected in your eyes and attitude what I want to think about myself. Why is that important? Then I have reinforcement for my reality and maybe I'll*

really be that way, or get what I want. Why is that important? Because I actually operate (down deep) from a place of low self-esteem and a sense of inadequacy. Where does that come from? My father belittled me continuously as a small child until I left home at 17. What are the implications? To survive emotionally, I made up a story that I'm better than most people. It is a serious over-compensation. It is unnecessary and even destructive in that it warps all my perceptions, feelings, and behavior. It interferes with all my human relationships and especially my relationship with myself. It is the cause of my grandiosity, my sense of entitlement, and fuels my inherent narcissism.

Not all of the fear analyses will be so detailed or necessarily so psychological. But if approached in prayer, we can get to the depths of what causes our fear. And to name them is to face them. This is the beginning of coming to God—full knowledge of our self-reliance and how ineffective it is ("... self-reliance failed us," BB page 68). The BB suggests self-reliance as the ultimate root of our fear. And it further suggests that God-reliance is the answer. Though absolutely correct, that answer doesn't give us the detail or the source of our personal fears ... so the naming and questioning exercise is important to see how self-reliance has manifested and to get in touch with its consequences.

The BB (page 68) also states that "we are in the world to play the role He assigns." Turn that statement into a question—what is the role God has assigned to you?

The answer is critical. "Just to the extent that we *do* as we think He would have us, and humbly rely on Him, does He enable us to match calamity with serenity." (BB page 68) Do you want inner peace? Figure out what God wants from you and do it! Place yourself in harmony with the Laws of the Universe, step into the Flow of the Universe as it unfolds.

"... we let Him demonstrate, through us, what He can do. We ask Him (pray) to remove our fear and direct our attention to what He would have us be." (BB page 68) This suggestion for prayer is a reminder that we're powerless over our fear. We can name it. We can analyze its causes and consequences. Then we pray for its removal. We trust infinite God—the decision that is the act of faith. God is Powerful; God is Caring; God is Present in my life. I made that decision in Step Two and reinforced that decision in Step Three: to have a personal relationship. This is the new basis of my reality: to trust and rely on God. I made the decision, now I'm going to act as if it's true. No matter what I know for sure, no matter how I feel right now—I'm going to act as if it is true: there is an all Powerful, all Caring, all Present God who knows my name and holds me in the palm of His hand.

You may find it productive to expand the fear analysis. After naming it and asking why we have it, we identify the specific behavior that results from it. We ask what the virtue opposite this fear would be and what behavior this would manifest. (See Appendix E 3 for worksheet.) This is an attempt to envision what might be a desired improvement.

P303

Rather than continuing to focus on the negative source of our fear, we create a positive vision of who we are being invited to become and how we are being invited to believe.

- **Sex**

So we come to a discussion of the third obstacle to a relationship with God. The BB has two primary themes as the basis of the sex inventory (pages 68–71): Let's have balance and use common sense; we each have a set of values deep down inside ourselves which need to be surfaced by this process and confirmed by God in prayer.

As with resentments and fear, once again we make a list—a head/heart/gut dump of names or incidents from our memory. Once we have this initial list, we review our history methodically (perhaps chronologically in buckets of time). When this list is complete we are ready for the analysis

The BB poses nine questions. Each of them is about our motives, the harm we may have done, and our responsibility in and for the situation:

1. Where had I been selfish?

2. Where had I been dishonest?

3. Where had I been inconsiderate?

4. Whom had I hurt?

5. Did I arouse jealousy?

6. Did I arouse suspicion?

7. Did I arouse bitterness?

8. Where was I at fault?

what was your motivation?

9. What should I have done instead?

See Appendix E 4 for worksheet.

p. 304

The answer to question 9 is the key. When we ask this question we measure our behavior by a standard, ideal, code, or value. We really do know what the appropriate course of action was for us personally. We feel guilt and shame when we violate these personal values. Guilt is a negative feeling about our behavior (what we did); shame is a negative feeling about our self (who we are).

The BB advises us to use the accumulated answers to question 9 to develop our sex ideal—that is, the principles for future sex behavior. Once again, we do this in prayer: "We asked God to mold our ideals ..." (BB page 69)

> This is not a process to describe an ideal partner relationship or sexual expectations. It's a process to identify personal values and confirm principles that will guide our future behavior with respect to sex.

AA does not impose any set of predetermined morals. In fact, the BB makes this very clear (pages 69 and 70):

- "We do not want to be the arbiter of anyone's sex conduct"

- "Whatever our ideal turns out to be, we must be willing to grow toward it"

- "We earnestly pray for the right ideal, for guidance in each questionable situation, for sanity, and for the strength to do the right thing."

My process yielded the following sex ideal:

I am a heterosexual man in a committed relationship. This requires fidelity, rigorous honesty, open-mindedness, and daily commitment. As a husband I am responsible to provide an environment in which my wife feels physically safe, financially secure, emotionally supported, and spiritually inspired. Together we are to pursue open communication, mutual goals, and responsible parenting. Our life together should be a balance of spiritual growth, work, fun, and pleasure.

The BB concludes the discussion by referring to our inventory as a list of our "grosser handicaps" (page 71). We are fishing for tuna, not minnows. This is not to be an exercise of self-obsession, but a nonjudgmental review of the major obstacles that manifest self-will and block us off from God.

This is a process of naming and beginning to remove the sludge that's accumulated over years during our self-centered efforts at survival, managing our own lives to the best of our ability. Our inventory describes in technicolor who we are and especially who we are not. This is our first venture into the promise of an awakened and accurate self-awareness and development of emotional sobriety.

We intuitively accept the adage that those who do not know and understand their history are condemned to repeat it. We begin to realize that we do not see or react to reality correctly. We also begin to accept the truth that we cannot change the past or control the future. But we do have responsibility for our own attitude, efforts, and behavior in the present.

> Through meetings (our Fellowship) we detox our body. Through the steps we detox our mind. Through service we detox our spirit.

Summary

Purpose	Identify the obstacles that block us from Power.
Instructions	Read and highlight:

1. Resentment BB pages 64–67

2. Fear BB pages 67–68

3. Sex BB pages 68–71

4. Step Four in the 12 & 12.

Process	Analyze behavior and identify our real motives.
Experience	

1. We are delusional; we're not who we think we are.

2. All our troubles are of our own making.

3. We can't see and accept the truth on our own power.

Result	Take responsibility for perceptions, feelings, reactions, and behavior. Pray and hold ourselves accountable.
Promise	Removal of the obstacles blocking us from God.

Reflection Questions

1. Have I sincerely asked God to reveal the truth to me?

2. Am I really open to the truth as whispered to me by the Spirit?

3. Have I been rigorously honest in each analysis of the motives underneath my behavior?

4. Do I take full responsibility for the troubles in my life? For my feelings? For my perceptions? For my behavior?

5. Am I willing to proceed to the full disclosure Step Five requires?

Be ready to do the next layer.

= energy

Meditation

I enter my interior space, noticing the darkness, the blocks, the brokenness. I ask the Spirit to hold these dark realities and help me to hold them with reverence and care. The Spirit's firm touch and reverent embrace transform them. The living waters of the Spirit's love wash over them.

I also notice the growing freedom in my interior space—not a freedom that dismisses brokenness, but a freedom that embraces my broken places and transforms me. I thank the Spirit for the darkness and the light, the woundedness and wholeness.

- Spirit of life-giving freedom, I ask for the grace of awareness of my own brokenness and darkness.
- Give me a willing and courageous spirit to delve deeply into my own vulnerability.
- Help me to see my areas of darkness so that these can come out into the light,
- to explore my brokenness so that it can respond to Your healing touch,
- to become aware of my resistances so that they can be freed by Your loving Spirit.

Help me be a resting place where others can bring their struggles as well as their joys.
Let me find a home in You so, through me, others can find their own path home.

Healing Spirit ... heal me.

5

Step Five

"Admitted to God, to ourselves, and to another human being the exact nature of our wrongs."

Prayer

Healing Spirit of the Universe.
    I cannot see that I do not see.
    I cannot hear that I do not hear.
    I do not know that I do not know.
Please:
    Open my eyes.
    Open my ears.
    Open my mind.
But especially open my heart:
    To really want to see;
    To really want to hear;
    To really want to know.
Allow me to accept at depth:
    My blindness;
    My deafness;
    My ignorance.
Please allow me to see, hear, and know the sources of
my brokenness in all their manifestations.

[handwritten annotations: "• yes or now? • then or now? "is it my "perception" that is broken? • am I whole but flawed or in need of healing?"]

Chapter Five

Reveal Obstacles to This Relationship

At this point in the step work, we have written out our story, analyzed the exact nature of our behavior (our motives, beliefs, and values), reviewed our guilt (for what we've done), and our shame (for who we are), and listed all our secrets.

Now what?

Bill Wilson and Dr. Bob Smith, as active members of the Oxford Group, studied the Letter of James from Christian scripture, which concludes: "If he has committed any sins, he will be forgiven. Therefore, confess your sins to one another and pray for one another that you may be healed."

The Oxford Group had "confession" as one of the six steps to a spiritual awakening. (BB page 263) Any such self-disclosure is a sacred process—one person revealing all, undefended, to another human being. The BB refers to it as a "life-and-death errand." (page 75)

> BB (page 25) states *"There is a solution.* Almost none of us liked the self-searching, the leveling of our pride, the confession of shortcomings which the process requires for its successful consummation."

Step Five is not therapy—although it will be therapeutic. Step Five is not a conversation—although both people will inevitably discuss some of the material. This is the time for full disclosure. We stand naked before God and another person—undefended. This is real intimacy—and this is not easy; "... a price had to be paid. It meant the destruction of self-centeredness." (BB page 14). The BB also suggests Step Five is a "humbling experience"; (page 72)—in fact, anyone who feels comfortable doing Step Five may not be doing it correctly.

A few guidelines for preparation follow:

- When you're close to completing Step Four, make an appointment for Step Five with the person you have chosen to hear it. The last thing you want is to finish Step Four and then have to wait a month or longer to do Step Five. It could get quite uncomfortable.

- Of course, you must have total confidence that the person hearing your Step Five confession is 100% trustworthy and that everything said will remain confidential.

- Doing Step Five in one sitting is ideal, though two- or three-hour segments also work. This is the first time for reviewing what you've written over the last several weeks or months (or perhaps even years!). And now you're not only seeing and reading it consecutively, but saying it out loud—hearing it for the first time. Over the several hours of reading, it makes quite an impression.

- Your sponsor/guide may want to choose the place. Be sure it guarantees privacy, has no possibility of interruption, and is comfortable—with everything you'll need.

My guide had, over the course of giving me the Step Four instructions, revealed aspects of his own life. I saw later that he was modeling for me the transparency called for in Step Five, while making me comfortable with self-exposure. He was also inspiring me to be rigorous, because his own story contained a relapse after 16 years which he attributed to a secret held in his Step Five. It became a cancer that eroded his sobriety slowly over a long period of time. The disease of alcoholism is very patient. Secrets shade us from the Sunlight of the Spirit. The Light grows dim and then gets blocked completely. And our dis-ease returns = obsession.

My experience with the Step Five process follows:

- As a way to begin, it may be helpful to review the BB instruction material on Step Five. For example, your sponsor/guide can read out loud the first paragraph on page 72; you can read the second paragraph, then you'll continue alternating until page 75: "We explain to our partner what we are about to do and why we have to do it." After answering these two questions, you'll finish reading that paragraph and the next: "We pocket our pride and go to it, illuminating every twist of character, every dark cranny of the past."

- Then it's time for you to read your inventory as written. The BB suggests that we be rigorously honest, turning

"Into Action"

over all the rocks to let the Sunlight of the Spirit shine in the dark places, on the exact nature of your behavior—not just recite the behavior. If new information or insights come to you while reading your inventory, share them with your guide and make notes so you can follow up as needed.

- You'll talk; your sponsor/guide will listen. If they need clarification, they can interrupt with a question or make notes (which are given to you when Step Five is finished).

- For each resentment for each person, institution, or principle, you'll have read the Column Three and Four analysis. At the end of the resentment portion of the inventory take a break to review observations and answer clarifying questions. Then you'll read your fear inventory, break and discuss, then your sex inventory and sex ideal, break and discuss.

- Once you finish reading the entire inventory, pick up the BB, open to page 75, and begin reading where you left off: "Once we have taken this step, withholding nothing ..." Your sponsor/guide will probably look you directly in the eyes and ask:

  1. *Did you write down everything that came to your consciousness about resentment, fear, sex? Have you kept any secrets?*

  The silence may be awkward. You've just spent several hours vocalizing your written Step Four—a process that has opened up your awareness to a point that allows the revelation of material you may have wanted to withhold. Grace is at work; willingness has been furnished.

2. *Did you read everything you wrote down?*

If you intentionally skipped over an embarrassing situation or detail, once again, Grace and willingness will move you to be complete, to reveal the total truth of self-deceit.

- Return to the BB (page 75) and read the Step Five promises:

"Once we have taken this step, withholding nothing, we are delighted. We can look the world in the eye. We can be alone at perfect peace and ease. Our fears fall from us. We begin to feel the nearness of our Creator. We may have had certain spiritual beliefs, but now we begin to have a spiritual experience. The feeling that the drink problem has disappeared will often come strongly. We feel we are on the Broad Highway, walking hand in hand with the Spirit of the Universe."

The final instructions are to go be alone and quiet for 60 minutes, reviewing what you've experienced. The BB suggests this review be done in prayer: "We thank God from the bottom of our heart that we know Him better." (BB page 75)

> Interesting ... you've spent several weeks or months writing out a personal inventory—all about yourself. Now you've just spent several hours reading it out loud—all about yourself. And the BB proclaims that as a result you know God better!

Step Five is a process to dismantle the false self and disintegrate the mask (persona) constructed in our attempts to cope with life's difficulties and our personal deficiencies. It's the roto-rooter that cleans out the sludge blocking the Sunlight of the Spirit. We then have direct access to the Light.

The BB suggests we review, in prayer, the work done in the first five steps—a reflection, a meditation. It's not a re-reading of our instructions or the Step Four work we've written, but a careful review of our process, asking the Spirit to reveal any details we've left out or additional work needed. It's not about being perfect; it is about being careful, as we build "an arch through which we shall walk a free man at last." (BB page 75)

> See Chapter Three of this book for the illustration of Bill Wilson's architectural analogy.

We can assume the building blocks of this arch include truths about exact causes and conditions, the very nature of our troubles: resentment, fear, sex, and by implication of the Step Five instructions, dishonesty and secrets—all manifestations of our self-centeredness. These building blocks are bound together by a powerful cement, made of our common peril (problem) as well as our common solution. (BB page 17)

Steps Four and Five are similar to ancient rites of passage in tribal cultures. Through this private process we may feel as though we have been initiated as authentic members in the Fellowship, placed solidly on a path of spiritual development, and introduced to a way of life that will return and foster our humanity. A new freedom indeed!

Some people suggest that after completing Step Five the person should burn or otherwise destroy their written Step Four inventory. This is not, in my experience, consistent with the BB's instruction. Later on the BB suggests making our Step Eight list of harms from the work done in Step Four. (BB page 76) I was instructed to keep my Step Four work until I'd finished Step Nine and then, in some ritualistic way meaningful to me, to get rid of it.

Summary

Purpose   Confess to another person the obstacles to our
              desired relationship with Power

Instructions Read and highlight:

              1. BB pages 72–75
              2. Step Five in the 12 & 12.

Process   Read Step Four inventory to someone,
              thoroughly revealing our shady behavior, our
              selfish motives, and our darkest secrets.

Experience   Some relief through catharsis; an
              overwhelming sense of brokenness and deep
              personal powerlessness.

Result   Feel hope based on complete self-revelation—
              an ability to look God in the face and accept
              compassion and forgiveness.

Promise   Beginning to have a spiritual experience, to
              know God better.

Reflection Questions

1. Have I been entirely honest (transparent) in Step Five?

2. Are there any areas of discomfort that I did not discuss with the person hearing my confession?

3. Do I need to talk to someone else about certain areas I've not discussed with my sponsor/guide?

4. What did I learn about myself through this process?

5. Do I really trust that God will forgive (has forgiven) me for my past?

6. Am I willing to forgive myself?

Meditation

Steps Four and Five are the beginning of a journey into emotional and spiritual maturity ...an initiation—a passage from the self-centered, self-obsessed way of the child.

We're on a journey into another way of life:

- A relationship with the source of Power, the Spirit of the Universe underlying the totality of things

- A relationship with our community of human beings with whom we share this journey.

We take responsibility for our thoughts.

We take responsibility for our feelings.

We take responsibility for our perceptions.

We take responsibility for our behavior.

We take responsibility for our lives: who we are; what we are; how we are.

We invite the Spirit to enter our lives and change our desert of loneliness into a garden of solitude.

To change our outward-reaching craving to an inward-reaching search.

To change our fearful clinging to fearless service.

To make real the soul math:

- The more I embrace God, the more of the true me is present

- The more I give away, the more I have.

Step Six

"Were entirely ready to have God remove all these defects of character."

Prayer

Creator, You know me, my history, the influences, both external and internal, that have made me who I am today. Please shine Your Light on my darkness so that the manifestations of my defects are revealed to me and I become willing to have them removed.

Chapter Six

Name Defects of Character

In stark contrast to the previous five steps, Step Six does not take a lot of time. The BB devotes one paragraph to it (page 76). The dominant themes are:

- We are ready to be changed

- God does the changing.

Once again, I made a list. Reviewing my inventory, most of my character defects were illustrated in living color.

My guide suggested I pray for sight:

- We cannot see that we do not see.

- We see what we know instead of knowing what we see.

Naming our character defects is another move to deflate ego at depth. When brought into the light, our shadows become our teachers. Naming them begins to take their power away. Some people may have a hard time identifying their character defects. They may actually see them not as flaws, but as necessary and desirable building blocks of their personality—the ingredients that make them who they are.

As a prompter, consider the Enneagram—a theory of personality based on three primary ways of receiving and reacting to reality: from the gut (1, 8, 9), heart (2, 3, 4), or head (5, 6, 7). Each type has three variations, giving us nine altogether—*ennea* in Greek. The following list (my own sorting) may be useful.

Enneagram—Some Defects of Character

Type 1 (gut)	Type 2 (heart)	Type 3 (heart)
Perfectionistic ✔	Proud ✓	Grandiose
Rigid/inflexible	Vainglorious	Arrogant
Critical/negative	Manipulative	Competitive ✓
Judgmental ✓	Smothering	Overachiever
Angry	Possessive	Image conscious
Intolerant	Needs others to	Insensitive
Bitter	depend on them	Feels worthless ✓
Anal	Has martyr	Chameleon
Impatient ✓	complex	/phony
Obsessive ✓	Hypochondriac	Self-deceiving
Rationalizing ✓	Needy	Jealous ✓
Controlling ✓	Resentful ✓	Dishonest
Tense	Negative	Lacks integrity
Disrespectful	Two-faced	Self-centered ✓
Fears being wrong ✓	Ungrateful	Driven
		Braggart
		Emotionally
		unavailable ✓
		Deceives others
		Irresponsible
		Fears failure ✓

Type 4 (heart)	Type 5 (head)	Type 6 (head)
Individualistic	Secretive	Lacks self-trust
Feels special	Removed/isolated	Fear based
Self-pitying	Cynical/skeptical	Slothful
Self-loathing/self-condemning	Detached	Fears being alone
	Loner	Rebellious
Dominated by feelings	Greedy (of time, resources, information)	Fears others
Envious	Eccentric	Self-doubting/unsure
Above the rule	Fearful	Passive-aggressive
Alienated from others	Dependent	Procrastinates
Moody	Antagonistic	Self-defeating
Aloof	Overly sensitive	Overreactive
Hopeless	Restless	Excitable
Victimized	Pessimistic	Anxious
Ungrateful	Emotionally needy	Miserly
Self-indulgent	Disdainful	Suspicious
Withdrawn	Non-supportive	Insecure
Harsh		Blaming
Remorseful		Defensive
Dependent		Pessimistic
Inhibited		

Type 7 (head)	Type 8 (gut)	Type 9 (gut)
Superficial	Hard hearted✓	Complacent
Easily bored	Ruthless	Stubborn ✓
Impulsive	Controlling ✓	Passive
Escapist	Aggressive	Neglectful
Restless/nervous	Lustful (sex,	Repressed
Fears deprivation	power)	Slothful
Glutton— ✓	Willful ✓	Fatalistic
compelled to fill	Intimidating	Denial
up with food /	Abusive	Aggressive
experience/etc.	Seeks/needs	Dependent
Hyper-active /	power	Given to fantasy
needs excitement	Violent	Self-neglect
Destructive	Fears being weak	Simplistic
Anxious	Independent ✓	Rigid
Irresponsible	Fears being	Compliant
Blaming	controlled ✓	Vicarious
Insecure	Self-centered ✓	Asleep
Overly dramatic	Fears fear	Self-deprecating
Materialistic	Proud ✓	Fickle
Undisciplined	Unaffectionate	Shallow
Self-centered ✓	Uncaring	Pessimistic
Needs immediate	Takes all the	Powerless
gratification	credit	Shunning
Reckless	Disrespectful	Fears change
	Impulsive	Inattentive
	Ruled by passion	Weak
	Unloving	Lazy ✓

131

Even those who have no problem making a list of character defects may be attached to them—fearing that without them they wouldn't be able to cope with life, succeed at work, manage their relationships. They cling to their defects believing they're necessary for survival.

The BB is clear that we need to be ready to have the defects removed. I've found the following exercise useful for visualizing what life would look like without them:

- Name the character defect

- Identify the resulting behavior

- Ask what's being defended

- Name the virtue that is the opposite of this specific defect

- Identify the behavior that flows from this virtue.

See this worksheet in Appendix F. (You also may want to revisit Appendix A's clinical description of narcissism.)

It doesn't take much analysis to uncover the delusion of a character defect's "value"—to see the benefit(s) of removing it and replacing it with its opposite.

The BB suggests that if we find ourselves unwilling to have a defect removed, we pray for the willingness. Once again, under each step is powerlessness—so we pray. We pray for sight; we pray for willingness. This is not a one-time prayer. We pray each day until we are entirely ready to be changed.

Because the list might be long it's useful to group defects into families for a better picture of patterns and impact, then eliminate duplicates. What I discovered is that the BB is wonderfully correct and simple. My character defects fell into four major classes:

- Resentment (fight)

- Fear (flight)

- Sex (dishonesty)

- Selfishness (self-obsession/narcissism).

So BB page 62 is exactly right: "Selfishness—self-centeredness! ... is the root of our troubles."

I was brought to a place of acute awareness that none of these is desirable, yet I saw a lifetime of sincere effort to eliminate or reduce them with very little success. I became deeply convinced that I was, and am, totally powerless over their removal or even their mitigation.

This concession brought me to a readiness for the intervention of Power.

We may need to revisit Step Two. What decision did I make about the attributes of God, the qualities I need my God to have? Does God have Power? Is God interested in my healing? Will God respond to my actions?

The Doctor's opinion suggests that our lives will be re-created (BB page xxviii); Step Three promises we'll be reborn. (BB page 63) Am I now willing to decide (act of my will) and to accept (act of my mind) that God can "now take them all—every one" (BB page 76)?

St. John of the Cross relates that "a bird is held in bondage just as well by a thread as by a rope."

An elephant trained to stay put by a chain around one leg affixed to a stake in the ground will eventually stay put with only the chain around the leg.

Summary

Purpose	Name defects of character
Instructions	Read and highlight:
	1. First paragraph of BB page 76
	2. Step Six from the 12 & 12.
Process	List character defects/shortcomings from Steps Four and Five; make a conscious and prayerful life review to reveal others.
Experience	Experience character defects distilled to their true nature.
Result	Feel humility: a deeper experience of personal powerlessness.
Promise	Possible elimination, or at least reduction, of character defects.

Reflection Questions

1. Are my character defects helping me or hurting me in my daily living?

2. What is the value or personal advantage of each of my character defects?

3. Am I really willing to be detached from them?

4. Do I really believe that God cares about me personally, will actually intervene in my life, and will change me?

5. Am I willing to be shown my true self?

6. Am I willing to be taken to a place I don't even know exists?

7. Do I feel safe with God?

Meditation

We sit in Loving Presence. Let It wash over and embrace us.

Healing Spirit, please wash away the blindness of our eyes, our hearts, and our minds so we can see ourselves as You see us.

Please reveal and transform blind spots that prevent us from facing the truth. Wash away the darkness and reveal the light of the truth.

Spirit of truth, enlighten our minds and hearts. Help us see that Your primary truth is that of overflowing love—that Your abundant love embraces both darkness and light, pain and joy, fear and courage, weakness and strength, defect and virtue, life and death.

Give us a heart like Yours—a heart that embraces brokenness and vulnerability, as You embrace them.

Thank You, Spirit of Light, for opening up our minds and hearts so we can be detached from the lie and be attached to the truth of who You are and who we are.

Thank You, Healing Spirit, for giving us the courage to embrace all aspects of ourselves and to want to receive Your healing.

7

Step Seven

"Humbly asked Him to remove our shortcomings."

Prayer

Healing Spirit of the Universe, I am tired of self-reliance.
Please inspire me to rely on You! Heal me in the ways that
will make me useful to You and others.

Please give me the desire to want less of me
and the yearning to have more of You.

Chapter Seven

Pray for Removal of Character Defects

Like Step Six, Step Seven has only one paragraph in the BB—page 76. Unlike Step Six, Step Seven has no instructions except as implied—it is a prayer.

As we look at Step Six and Step Seven we see the terms "defects of character" and "shortcomings" used. I've heard various explanations of the differences; however, I've also heard a tape where Bill Wilson responded with a slight laugh: "Oh, I was taught to never use the same word or phrase in consecutive sentences. There is no difference." So much for speculation on different meaning, intent, or nuance.

This paragraph on BB page 76 asks us, when ready to have our character defects/shortcomings removed, to pray. Once again, the assumption underneath this request is that we are powerless and must rely on Power.

The prayer begins "My Creator ..."

Each of us is made a certain way: with a specific heritage, DNA hardwiring, cultural/familial conditioning, level of intelligence, education, etc. My story included spending lots of money and time to have insight and to change. I tried everything from religion to psychology to self-help programs to drugs and fasting, vitamins and aerobics ... and finally even AA. I was not touched. Oh, I obtained a lot of information. I got quite physically healthy. I even had my addiction to alcohol removed (notice, I do not claim sobriety in the first four years—just abstinence from alcohol). All this resulted in my narcissism being even more vigorous—with a sharper edge for manipulating all those around me to serve my needs.

However, in spite of these self-accomplishments, I did not change! Actually, I was able to operate with a more grandiose delusion—I fancied myself a true renaissance man. I did not see that I did not know that I did not know. Yet I was a Neanderthal using my information and skills to use and abuse all those with whom I came in contact.

In 1988, when I finished Step Six and was brought to Step Seven, my guide asked me to write out my own Step Seven prayer based on the principles of the BB page 76 prayer. As with the similar instruction for the Step Three prayer, this was not to improve upon the prayer, but to understand it by paraphrasing the original.

"My Creator "	I need to be re-created.
"I am now willing "	From the Step Six exercise.
"that you should have all of me good and bad."	Which reinforces the Step Three surrender of my will and my life (100%).
"I pray that you now remove from me "	A request of soul surgery by the Divine Healer; an act of exorcism: the removal of the bedevilments (see BB page 52).
"every single defect of character "	Connection to Step Six.

"which stands in the way of my usefulness to you and my fellows."	Note this is not about me feeling good, being good, or being comfortable /happy/successful. It's about the removal of the obstacles in me that prevent the flow of God's life (Grace) through me out to others.
"Grant me strength "	I am powerless and in desperate need for Power.
"as I go out from here to do your bidding."	My will (decision) is to align my will with my vision (the conclusion of my thinking) of God's will and to take the indicated action (through use of my body in trust).

"Amen."

This is the end of this phase of the step process that began with Step Four—dealing with relation with self:

- Step Four
- Step Five
- Step Six

- Name the obstacles
- Reveal them to another human being
- Name the character defects that come from these manifestations of self

- Step Seven
- Concede that a Power other than myself or other human powers is absolutely necessary to remove the defects.

Then, on my knees, I prayed my own Step Seven prayer and the original BB prayer.

Although I knew that I had completed Step Seven and all the preceding work to the best of my ability, I also was aware that my over-arching character defect had not been removed. I was very disheartened. This defect was eroding my professional life, my personal life, and as the BB promises on page 70—it would eventually undermine my program.

It dominated me and I was desperate. On Thursday night at my men's BB step group a man shared that he prayed to have a specific character defect removed. I heard that and knew it wasn't in the BB or the 12 & 12; however, I also heard that this was his actual experience and that it had worked.

On Saturday (I thought about it for two days—no sense rushing into these things!), I went into my bedroom, shut the door, got on my knees, and centered myself in the presence of the Power I had begun to experience due to the work of the previous steps (as promised in the BB). I was about to pray the Step Seven prayer for the removal of this specific character defect. I stopped. I was startled. An awareness arose in me of pure unwillingness, absolute resistance—I recognized I was viscerally attached to this character defect and the behavior it manifested. Again I was shocked. After months of very thorough Step Four work, a lengthy Step Five of complete transparency, and a Step Six where I believed I was completely ready to be changed—here I was completely unwilling.

Then, as the BB suggests in Step Six, I prayed for the willingness to be willing.

Immediately I called my guide to proudly recount this epiphany. He listened quietly and when I finished he gently said, "That's a wonderful insight, Herb; now stop the behavior." WOW! I got it. Another awakening. *I have no power over the character defect, but I have responsibility for how it manifests in behavior.*

I began a daily regimen of prayer and accountability:

- Prayer: daily asking for the removal of this specific character defect

- Accountability: daily calling my guide (and also my sponsor) to reveal exactly what I was thinking, feeling, and doing with respect to this character defect.

My goal was complete transparency. Immediately the power of the defect diminished; over the next several days and weeks it was removed and has not returned.

> Prayer and accountability are a powerful
> process and effective tool.

Dr. Jim Finley, my spiritual director, commented in a retreat he led:

> "We hold onto our identity as our security, and it is in the willingness to let go of these illusions that we find our true self and ultimate freedom."

Richard Rohr (a Franciscan priest) wisely says that our character defects are either transformed or we transmit them.

Step Seven on BB page 76 begins "Humbly ..." The 12 & 12, Step Seven, has a wonderful commentary on humility. What is humility? It comes from the Latin word "humus" which means earth: common as dirt, having no particular distinction. St. Theresa of Avila (sixteenth century mystic) says that humility is truth. My sponsor says humility is when your outside and inside match.

I was reading the Rule of St. Benedict (the basis of the monastic movement begun in the sixth century). St. Benedict articulates 12 steps to humility. I could not resist summarizing them here:

1. Be conscious of the reality of God (awe)

2. Avoid self-will

3. Follow direction

4. Accept life as it manifests (patience/endurance)

5. Be transparent (no secrets)

6. Have no complaints (acceptance)

7. Diminish your "self"

8. Be one of many, do not stand out (be ordinary)

9. Observe silence (unless spoken to)

10. Practice decorum; no unnecessary frivolity

11. Speak appropriately: gentle, brief, restrained

12. Be modest of demeanor (recollection; measured response).

These suggestions speak to all of us who aspire to a more spiritual way of life.

"In humility is perfect freedom because in humility we accept the truth" (Thomas Merton).

Summary

Purpose   Remove or reduce defects of character

Instructions   Read and highlight:

1. Second paragraph of BB page 76

2. Step Seven in the 12 & 12.

Process   Pray the Step Seven prayer specifically for the removal of individual defects of character, no matter how resistant you feel.

Experience   Willingness to pray for the removal of a specific shortcoming, to be conscious of it; willingness to stop the behavior that is a manifestation of it, and to be accountable daily to my sponsor and/or guide for the results.

Result   Change behavior

Promise   Removal or mitigation of character defects.

Reflection Questions

1. Am I willing to be held accountable (transparency with my sponsor and/or guide) for my behavior?

2. What does humility mean for me?

3. Am I willing to seek humility, to pray for it?

4. What virtues would I like to manifest?

5. How big (Powerful) is my God?

Meditation

O persistent God, deliver me from assuming your mercy is gentle.

Pressure me that I may grow more human, not through the lessening of my struggles, but through an expansion of them that will undamn me and unbury my gifts.

Deepen my hurt until I learn to share it and myself openly and my needs honestly.

Sharpen my fears until I name them and release the power I have locked in them and they in me.

Accentuate my confusion until I shed those grandiose expectations that divert me from the small, glad gifts of the now, and the here, and the me.

Expose my shame where it shivers, crouched behind the curtains of propriety, until I can laugh at last through my common frailties and failures, laugh my way toward becoming whole.

Deliver me from just going through the motions and wasting everything I have which is today, a chance, a choice, my creativity, your call.

O persistent God, let how much it all matters pry me off dead center so if I am moved inside to tears, or sighs, or screams, or smiles, or dreams, they will be real. And I will be in touch with who I am, and who you are, and who my sisters and brothers are.

-Source Unknown

8

Step Eight

"Made a list of all persons we had harmed, and became willing to make amends to them all."

Prayer

We are on a high road to a new freedom.
But freedom requires forgiveness:
    Forgiveness is our release of others;
    Forgiveness is our release of ourselves.

But forgiveness in turn requires repentance:
    Repentance happens by naming of our character defects
    through inventory and the changing of our behavior
    through amends.

But repentance requires Power because we're powerless:
    Powerless to see;
    Powerless to change.

And access to Power requires prayer;

And prayer is a decision—to believe in, to surrender to, and
to live in the Presence of God.

In that Presence let us
    Evaluate our yesterdays,
    Prepare for tomorrow,
    And especially live in our today.

Chapter Eight

Name Harm Done to Others

Steps One, Two, and Three establish our relationship with God. Steps Four, Five, Six, and Seven rehabilitate our relationship with our true self. Steps Eight, Nine, and Ten address our relationships with the broad community of humanity.

Step Eight is the process of naming people and institutions we've harmed and what we did so we can take corrective action to repair the damage through Step Nine. Step Ten is a spiritual tool to keep the channel of Grace in us clear of resentment, fear, dishonesty, and selfishness—impediments to the Light.

Now, for Step Eight, we are asked to make another list. The BB states we began this process when we prepared our Step Four inventory. Since Step Four is about resentment, fear, and sex, it's a good start. But there are people we've harmed in other ways: accidents, ignoring, dishonesty, etc. who should be listed, even though there is no resentment. Harm can be caused by actions we took or actions we failed to take. We are becoming acutely aware that we are powerless to really know and accurately name the harm we've done. So we pray. Once again the BB suggests that "we ask ..." (page 76) even just for the willingness.

The BB descriptions of Steps Eight and Nine are connected and recognize this phase of the process is difficult. It reminds us of the instruction leading up to Step Three: "If you have decided you want what we have and are willing to go to any length to get it—then you are ready to take certain steps." (BB page 58) Now, the BB instructions encourage us twice to remember why we are doing what we are asked to do in Step Nine.

> - "Remember it was agreed at the beginning *we would go to any lengths for victory over alcohol.*" (BB page 76)
>
> - "Reminding ourselves that we have decided to go to any lengths to find a spiritual experience ..." (BB page 79)

Note how this addresses both halves of Step One:

- Alcohol—the symptom of the problem

- Unmanageability—the spiritual malady (underlying nature of the problem) that requires a spiritual solution.

Again on page 79 the BB wants us to acknowledge our powerlessness to do this. "... we ask that we be given strength and direction to do the right thing, no matter what the personal consequences may be."

The focus of Step Eight is naming harm (damage or injury). The BB and the 12 & 12 also use synonyms like hurt, hate, dislike, wrong, criminal, betray, depress, disturb; I use the word diminish. How did I diminish others ... directly or indirectly:

- Physically—body?

- Financially—money/value/property?

- Mentally—lie/distortion of reality?

- Emotionally—stress/peace/security?

- Spiritually—relationship with God?

One of my friends uses the seven key words from the resentment inventory: How did I harm a person's self-esteem, pride, ambition, security, personal relations, sex relations, or pocketbook?

The 12 & 12 chapter on Step Eight suggests we review our entire life and our relationships with others:

- Taking an accurate and unsparing survey of our past life

- Completing a deep and honest search of our motives and actions

- Naming the flaws in our makeup

- Listing the personality traits that disturb and injure others

- Becoming aware of our basic instincts and how they bring us into collision with others.

During this review it may become clear that other people have harmed us—perhaps more devastatingly than we have harmed them. However, once again, as with Column Four of the resentment inventory, we look only at *our* behavior, *our* motives, the energy and impact that flowed from *us* toward them. Their role, their behavior, is none of our business: "… we are trying to put our lives in order." (BB page 77) Indeed, but this is not the heart of the matter. "Our real purpose is to fit ourselves to be of maximum service to God and the people about us." (BB page 77) This is more of the turning—from self to OTHER/others.

So we make our list. In prayer we listen, take direction, and try to be objective.

I used 3 x 5 cards; they make it easier to sort, correct, and track. On each card I wrote:

1. Name of person harmed

2. Harms done (behavior and impact)

3. The amend I believed was appropriate and required

4. Contact information (phone number, address, email)

5. Whether I was willing or unwilling to make the amend, at this time.

The details are important. The more specific we are about the harm, the more relevant will be the amend. As with a tooth cavity, the dentist will drill out all the disease before applying the filling.

When I was finished and had completed my Step Eight list and the 3x5 cards, I called my sponsor/guide for an appointment to review them. His key question "where is the harm?," filtered out those where I felt guilt or shame but had not created any harm. Because I resented someone doesn't mean I harmed them. Because I talked badly about someone (gossip) doesn't mean I harmed them. He pointed out that I'm really not that important or powerful and asked if the person gossiped about had really lost money, job, opportunity, reputation, or friends as the result of my actions. Usually the answer was no. He suggested that the person harmed may have been the person I gossiped *to* rather than about.

What about putting yourself on the list of people harmed? The BB page 66 states "Sometimes it was remorse and we were sore at ourselves." This seems to imply that we have resentments directed toward ourselves and we are certainly very aware that we've created tremendous damage to ourselves emotionally, financially, physically, mentally, and especially spiritually. However, as spiritually sick people we are always putting ourselves first. So if you need to review how you've harmed yourself, be last on the list. The very process of doing the steps, especially Step Nine, is the biggest amend (personal change and reparation to others) you can do for yourself—to be restored to your own humanity.

> This is not self-help, but a spiritual process of receiving God's help.

My sponsor/guide also helped me sort out:

- Whether to make the amends or to let it go and not intrude in their lives. We discussed each one; some of those I wanted to see he suggested that I not see— indicating my ego (or other character defect) may be motivating me. Some I felt I should not see; he proposed I see them because my fear may be motivating me. If a decision was made not to see them, he helped me clarify what action would complete the amend process.

- The appropriate amend. He helped me be specific and suggested that if I didn't know what amend would satisfy the situation, I should ask the person harmed.

- Whether to make a direct amend (face to face) or indirect amend (telephone or letter).

My sponsor/guide reviewed with me the attitude I needed when preparing to make these amends: to be helpful and forgiving:

- To be helpful ...   to restore what was taken away or to provide an opportunity for the person to heal. If they were unaware of the harm (such as unknown infidelity), he endorsed the BB's suggestions that we not discuss it.

- To be forgiving ... to   release   others   and   to   be released.

> Release = to relieve from obligation; to set free.

No single direction or even series of examples can possibly fit the variety of conditions and situations for all people. Just remember the primary guiding principle is that we are not to create harm through our amends, and we are not to get free at another's expense. He reminded me that this process is not necessarily to make me feel good, but to continue the deflation of my ego.

These cards were to become my road map, telling me where I was at all times and holding me specifically accountable to where I was going. I was able to set priorities. I decided to do the easier ones first, to get a rhythm and develop comfort. Besides, I truly believe that the completion of each amend generates power. And some of the more difficult ones required a lot of Power—not mine.

I dated the cards so I knew what was completed, what was outstanding, and when I was balking (and for how long). My sponsor/guide referred me to others when he didn't have experience with how to right a wrong—for example, with the law (attorneys), IRS (accountants), etc.

Now about forgiveness.

Forgiveness is *not* to:

- Condone
- Forget
- Tolerate
- Ignore
- Approve

- Excuse
- Minimize
- Pardon
- Deny
- Absolve

- Reconcile
- Invite to hurt again
- Surrender justice
- Feel good
- Befriend

Forgiveness is a *decision* to not:
- Retaliate
- Exact revenge
- Seek compensation
- Judge
- Resent
- Fear

Forgiveness is a *decision* to:
- Release them
- Release ourselves
- Be released.

Forgiveness is not a decision made in isolation, but a process that begins way back with Column Three of the resentment inventory, where we identify our delusional beliefs about who we are and are not, who others are, and how the world works. It continues with Column Four where we see clearly to what extent we are, or are not, responsible for the event itself but are 100% responsible for our perception and reaction to it as well as our behavior around it. As part of this responsibility we see and accept that we are, or have been, spiritually sick, blind to our role, powerless to fix ourselves, but capable of prayer for our own healing.

In Step Five we went public (with at least one person); in Steps Six and Seven we once again accepted our powerlessness and continued our prayer for healing. Now in Step Eight we take responsibility for our part in hurting them and also in remaining sick ourselves by not taking the necessary healing action. We acknowledge and accept our powerlessness to have done any differently and release them and/or ourselves from this hurt. So once again we pray for Power—to see, to accept, and especially to heal and be healed through forgiveness.

In the Our Father we ask to be forgiven just to the extent that we forgive others. In the prayer of transformation,　St. Francis suggests: "It is by forgiving that one is forgiven." Several excellent books address the importance and the process of forgiveness, such as :

- Fred Luskin (clinical psychologist), *Forgive for Good*
- Patrick Brennan (Catholic priest), *The Way of Forgiveness.*

Everything we want is on the other side of Step Nine!

Summary

Purpose   Identify all we have harmed and what we did

Instructions   Read and highlight:

    1. BB pages 76–84

    2. Step Eight in the 12 & 12.

Process   Make a list:

    People and institutions harmed

    Harms done (be specific)

    Suggested amend

    Contact information

    Indication of willingness or unwillingness to amend.

    Pray where unwilling.

Experience   List reviewed with sponsor or guide.

Result   Prepare a specific list and a specific plan.

Promise   Readiness to have a new way of life and to experience real freedom.

Reflection Questions

1. Am I willing to address/repair the harms that I've done to others?

2. Have I reviewed my list with my sponsor/guide, been rigorously honest, and taken direction?

3. If I find myself unwilling in any area, am I at least willing to pray for the willingness and hold myself accountable about this unwillingness?

4. Am I willing to forgive all those who harmed me ... to release every single one of them?

5. Am I willing to pray for the healing of all those I've harmed?

6. Am I really ready and willing to be released, to be healed?

Meditation

We open our minds, memories, and hearts to remember the hurts, the wounds, where and when we've been dishonored, abused, lied to, cheated on, diminished in spirit and emotion, let down, harmed physically or financially.

We bring to our minds, memories, and hearts a picture of the betrayer: father or mother, husband or wife, boyfriend or girlfriend, brother or sister, relative or friend, school, church, judicial system, healthcare system, legal system, government.

This is the reality—it did happen—we have been betrayed, hurt and deeply wounded. Name it and accept it. It is tragic and it is true.

It is also true that we can be healed from these wounds.

- To forgive is not to condone or excuse the behavior. What was done was wrong.

- To forgive is not to pardon—that's not ours to give; we don't have the power of absolution.

- To forgive is not to forget. We are saddened by the memory and must grieve the event.

- To forgive is to release from debt; to release from the demand for retribution or retaliation.

- To forgive is to surrender the right to get even.

(con't)

The reality is that as long as we hold onto these hurts, they possess us; actually they poison us emotionally and spiritually.

To forgive is to take responsibility for our part, which may only be that we have been holding onto these memories and feelings—allowing them to continue devastating our emotional and our spiritual life.

How long are we going to carry these wounds? How long are we going to be shackled by the chain towing this garbage barge of hurt, anger, and shame?

All spiritual traditions believe that we are forgiven just to the extent that we forgive; all spiritual traditions believe that we are released just to the extent that we release others.

Look at our own brokenness—the many betrayals for which we have been responsible. Look at our motives, our role, in the events where we find ourselves betrayed. Where were we selfish, dishonest, angry, or afraid?

In light of our own brokenness, look at *their* brokenness—see them like us—those who hurt us are themselves hurt, fearful, wounded, sick people—human beings twisted by their own personal histories.

We are all weak, wounded human beings, full of defects— attempting to survive the difficulties of life and find a little peace and happiness.

Forgiveness is the release of others and the harm they have caused us. But forgiveness often follows deep acceptance of and repentance for our own harmful actions to others.

(con't)

We are powerless to name and accept the truth of the harm we have done; we are likewise powerless to release the hurt others have done to us.

- Are we willing to pray for the power:

  - to ask for knowledge of the truth?

  - to ask for freedom from the bondage of our own history?

  - to wish for the spiritual healing of persons or institutions that have harmed us?

  - to forgive ourselves?

  - to let go of self-condemnation, remorse, our temper, our addictions, our vanities, our arrogance, our smugness, and our failures to do what we must and be who we are?

- Are we willing to pray for the power:

  - to love them as we love ourselves?

  - to see the world and the people in it from God's point of view?

We are beginning a process of personal forgiveness and reconciliation.

Invite the healing Power of the universe:

- Into our minds—that our memories may be healed

- Into our hearts—that our feelings may be healed

- Into our soul—that our human spirit may be healed and that it may flourish. (con't)

Healing Spirit of the universe:

- Enable us to be willing to let go, to forgive, to release
- Enable us to be willing to find freedom
- Enable us to be willing to be restored to sanity
- Enable us to be willing to be taken to a place of serenity.

Holy Spirit, breathe your Spirit into us.

9

Step Nine

"Made direct amends to such people wherever possible except when to do so would injure them or others."

Prayer

Forgiving Spirit of the Universe:
Grant us the courage to approach those we have harmed
and to speak to them in such a way that they are released
from the bondage of that harm. Heal them at the deepest
level and allow them to forgive us.

Give us the willingness to change behavior and to be
changed in attitude. Heal us at the deepest level and allow
us to want and pursue a life of helpful service.

Chapter Nine

Make Amends: Personal Change and Reparation to Others

"Amend" means two primary actions:
1. To change attitude, and especially behavior
2. To repair damage caused to others.

Bill Wilson and the first group of recovered alcoholics clearly understood both the importance and the difficulty of Step Nine. As discussed in this book's Chapter Eight, the BB reminds us twice of our original commitment *to go to any length.* Commenting on the Traditions, Bill Wilson said they are not rules or regulations, but are the accumulated wisdom of our collective experience. He said we do not need rules and regulations. There are only two disciplines in AA: one is alcohol; the other is God. The alcoholic will be ruled by one or the OTHER. The final step in the turning process is Step Nine—the first step that requires really getting outside our comfort zone.

The previous steps were essentially done by ourselves, except Step Five which is completed with a trusted confidante. Now Step Nine has us go to those we've harmed, acknowledge the harm specifically, take responsibility for our part (and not discuss *their* contribution to the event), and clean it up—repairing the damage as best we can. Remember the purpose of the Steps is deflation of ego at depth, so that room is made for God. Step Nine is intended to be very humbling—the final step in "... the destruction of self-centeredness." (BB page 14)

The BB commits eight pages to underlying principles and attitude for our amends and gives several examples. It talks about facing the individuals harmed, or calling, or writing a letter, or making a decision not to contact the harmed individual at all. It also talks about the probability of not being able to find everyone on our list. It discusses the attitude we should take in the approach, emphasizes actions rather than words, and states: "A remorseful mumbling that we are sorry won't fill the bill at all." (BB page 83)

Principles for amends:

- To be of maximum service

- To carry a beneficial message

- To provide a demonstration of good will

- To intend prayer-full God reliance.

Attitudes for amends:

- Tact, common sense, consideration, humility

- Helpful and forgiving spirit

- Regret and willingness for reparation

- Calm, frank, open, direct, and honest demeanor

- Loving kindness, patience, tolerance.

I was given a simple process: to call and make an appointment with each person listed on one of the cards from Step Eight. I started with the easiest ones. Sometimes I met them at a coffee shop, sometimes in a park, sometimes at their home; circumstances dictated the appropriate venue. I rarely did it over a meal at a restaurant—too much potential for interruption, and not enough privacy for honest reaction.

When I was sitting across from the individual I told them why I was there. Usually I said "Periodically, I review my life to determine if I've harmed anybody and your name came to mind." I discussed alcoholism and my spiritual efforts only if appropriate and useful to the person and the conversation.

The process is quite specific:

1. Tell the person the harm as remembered— focused and to the point. No excuses.

2. Ask the person if they would like to comment on how the behavior affected them and/or if there are any other harms. Then be silent and wait. The person (especially if they are not in a Twelve-Step program or on a spiritual path) is usually quite uncomfortable with the process and especially with the silence. Listen carefully if the person responds; if no response within 30 to 60 seconds, take it to the next phase.

3. Suggest an appropriate amend (some action proportionate to or commensurate with the harm done).

4.   Ask the person to comment on the acceptability of the suggested amend and/or if any other actions need to be taken to repair the damage. Again remain silent for 30 to 60 seconds, allowing them time to process and respond.

All those who have made amends, under the direction of an experienced sponsor/guide, have experienced miracles. Yes, miracles: a wonder, a supernatural event, a you-can't-get-here-from-there experience.

Some personal experiences:

- In 1965 I had misused my best friend's motorcycle and lied about the damage. In 1989, when he returned to this country and we were having dinner, I acknowledged this harm. Not only did he accept my apology but he indicated he would appreciate it if I would take his current motorcycle; it was in storage, since his travels didn't allow time for it.

> I made an amend about a motorcycle and I ended up with a motorcycle. (I paid him market value even though he wanted to give it to me.)

- I made an appointment with the Executive Vice President of a firm I used to work for to make restitution for stealing through misuse of my expense account over several years. He was impressed with my honesty, commented that they had underpaid me, agreed to call it even. Then he asked if I needed a letter from him to AA.

I chuckled and declined the letter.

- I was on retreat at Ghost Ranch out in the middle of the vast New Mexico desert. After preparing individual amends cards for three dead people I had harmed, and making a firm resolution to visit a local cemetery when I returned to Los Angeles, I took a walk into the desert. About 30 minutes on the trail I noticed the sunlight glinting off an object 20 yards from the trail. I was curious and left the trail to investigate. When I got to the source of the reflection, I discovered three tombstones.

I was able to make my three amends then and there.

- A woman I recruited into my firm and mentored for years eventually became my boss. Because of my inappropriate behavior at work she was required to force me to resign and leave the company I had been with for 21 years. (I was four years sober in AA but I had not done the Steps and had not changed). In 1988, after doing the Steps and becoming aware of and taking responsibility for my work behavior, I met with her to make my amends. We had a wonderful two hours where we both acknowledged our respective roles and we were totally reconciled. And it's a good thing—she later married my sponsor!

> Our relationship was so healed that when she decided to convert to Catholicism she asked me to be her Confirmation sponsor.

You can't get here from there!

- I needed to make an amend to a woman for some harmful behavior two decades previous. My guide said he had no experience with whether it was appropriate to contact her after so many years and suggested I talk to a woman in the program whose experience I trusted. She said to call the other woman, who was glad to hear from me and relieved to be able to receive my amends. I could tell a healing in her was taking place as we talked.

> She became free of the memory. I became free of the guilt and shame.

- I spent special time with each of my three children. They are not shy and are quite verbal. We had long amend talks. Today they love to come to our house, especially on holidays, and frequently stay overnight—with spouses, grandkids, dogs.

> We are good friends and I am a trusted parent, role model, mentor, and now grandparent.

- My father was dead 12 years. I had done tons of therapy, retreats, men's groups, Life Springs, and other self-help exercises, etc. to resolve my anger toward him. No relief. In 1988, for my Step Nine, I was directed to go to a cemetery close by to make my amends. I took a blanket to sit on, water to drink, a notebook to write in, and a box of tissues (I'm a crier). I prayed that my heart be opened and that my dad's spirit be present. Then I wrote him a letter as if he were there to receive it. I read it to him—out loud. We talked. I listened. I laughed and I cried.

> When I walked out of the cemetery two hours later, I was free. We were reconciled. I am still sad for our history, but I am no longer angry. I have a compassion for his life I never had before.

- My mother and I had a disagreement concerning money just before I got sober. She said loan; I understood gift. After I got sober, I paid the money back. She was so angry over the situation she sold her home, moved out of town, and did not leave a forwarding address.

In 1988 I resolved to try to make amends, so I wrote a letter. But I had no address. However, I knew she got a pension check. So I contacted the pension administrator and asked them to forward my letter. They did. In it I acknowledged my fault and offered to be of help in any way she felt that I could make her life more comfortable. I sent pictures of her three grandchildren (she had been very close to them, but hadn't seen them in four years). In a couple of weeks the letter was returned. It had been opened and read. But she was still so angry that the pictures of the children were returned. No word for about two years. Then a phone call asking if my offer to help was still good. She had terminal lung cancer ... six months to live. We brought her home, gently re-established our relationship, used our resources to support her illness, visited her every day in the last month. My wife and I helped her die with dignity, fully reconciled with her entire family.

- In 1988 I sat with my wife of 22 years and had several long talks. I acknowledged my insensitivity, the emotional damage I had inflicted, my financial irresponsibilities, and the personal betrayal. (I followed the BB suggestions [pages 69 and 81] and the counsel of my sponsor, guide, and therapist.)

We each acknowledged that we were powerless to fix our marriage, that we were powerless to even discern whether we wanted to stay together. (She's also in a Twelve-Step program, has a sponsor, and is following a spiritual path.)

We decided to stop talking about our marriage, our relationship, our history, and our future. We stopped going to marriage counseling. We stopped reading books on marriage. We decided to start really working on our respective individual spiritual development and to seek psychological support. Our purpose: to get clear on the fundamentals of being a human being with a clear and honest relationship with ourselves as individuals.

And being convinced of our powerlessness to decide whether to stay together, we agreed to pray together. Each morning we would kneel, face each other, hold hands, look each other in the eyes, and pray out loud. We did not pray to stay; we did not pray to leave. We prayed for our individual healing and the guidance as to what to do. One morning she would pray out loud; the next morning would be my turn to pray out loud. A spontaneous, short prayer—30 seconds, for healing.

Well, you can't get on your knees, face each other, hold hands, look into each other's eyes and pray out loud for healing and stay mad. Our anger began to subside. The attitudes began to soften. The behavior became more conciliatory. We began to re-establish our friendship.

We did this prayer practice for at least three years.

Today we're good friends. We don't have a perfect marriage (whatever that is) but we do have a shared life—with common values, a passion for our families, and an enjoyment that bubbles over into our work and our community in the form of fun and service. We enjoy being who we are individually and being with each other as a couple. Our lives individually and as a couple flourish.

- There are people I can't find (for a variety of reasons). I take each into prayer and determine with God's guidance and the direction of my sponsor/guide what I should do about each amend situation. An example: as part of my reparation to women in general, I accepted an invitation to support a women's recovery home in my area (I'm not involved with the women; I am involved in forming business policies and fund-raising).

We need to be creative and persistent in our approach to making amends.

I have completed *all* my amends. Yes, we <u>can</u> *finish* all our amends.

> Just because they ask doesn't mean we have to comply.

Remember that we are sometimes dealing with spiritually and emotionally sick people. Although the final phase of the amends process is to ask if there's anything else we need to do to make it right, that doesn't mean we have to do it if it doesn't make sense.

A man I worked with had been divorced 20 years but still needed to make amends for the stress he caused his ex-wife. They had not talked in years. She wouldn't respond to his phone calls. I suggested that he write a letter and have me review the draft before he sent it. She responded within a week; they set up an appointment. He met with her, followed the recommended process, and asked if there was anything else he could do. Without hesitation she asked him to write a check for $25,000. He blinked, caught his breath, and had the good sense to respond "I'll get back to you." After reviewing with me the circumstances surrounding the divorce 20 years earlier, the property settlement, the alimony, the child support, etc., we determined (in prayer) that he was clean. He did not owe her any money. He called her and told her he would not be sending additional money. She was holding him hostage and trying to use emotional blackmail to take advantage of any guilt. His amend was complete.

We hear a lot about "living" amends. If that means we change our attitude and our behavior (or continuously make efforts to), it's okay. However, if it is a substitute for consciously and directly addressing the person harmed, it's not at all okay! Human beings (especially those affected by alcoholism) are too susceptible to rationalization and the easier, softer way.

A major intended result of this Step Nine process is deflation of our ego at depth, to give us a humbling experience. We will feel uncomfortable, and may suffer pain (financial, disgust, embarrassment) or even prison.

- Are we willing to go to any lengths for our freedom:
  - From alcohol?
  - From our unmanageability; our spiritual malady; our cancer of the soul?

- Are we willing to have a spiritual experience/awakening:
  - To be completely transformed?
  - To be changed?

- To be taken to a place we don't even know exists?
- To become a person we've never known or experienced?
- To live a life that's never been available to us?
- To be comfortable within our own skin?
- To have our life really flourish and be filled with meaning?

"If we are painstaking about this phase of our development ..." (painstaking: diligent with details), these are the promises (BB pages 83 and 84):

1. We will be amazed before we are half-way through.
2. We are going to know a new freedom and a new happiness.
3. We will not regret the past, nor wish to shut the door on it.
4. We will comprehend the word serenity and we will know peace.
5. No matter how far down the scale we have gone, we will see how our experience can benefit others.
6. That feeling of uselessness and self-pity will disappear.
7. We will lose interest in selfish things and gain interest in our fellows.
8. Self-seeking will slip away.
9. Our whole attitude and outlook will change.
10. Fear of people and of economic insecurity will leave us.
11. We will intuitively know how to handle situations that used to baffle us.
12. We will suddenly realize that God is doing for us what we could not do for ourselves.

These are the promises that manifest in our lives after completing Steps Two through Nine—the process of spiritual transformation. Contrast them with the Step One promises of the spiritual malady as revealed in the paragraph on BB page 52—the bedevilments.

We have truly experienced a kind of exorcism.

The BB boldly states that these are not extravagant promises, "… that they will always materialize if we work for them." (BB page 84)

Summary

Purpose	Become useful to God and others through amends
Instructions	1. Read and highlight:
	- BB pages 76–84
	- Step Nine in the 12 & 12
	2. Under guidance of a sponsor/guide, begin making amends.
	3. Receive and do assignments on Steps Ten, Eleven, and Twelve.
Process	After review with our guide, meet with (or contact) each harmed person or institution:
	1. Tell them the harm
	2. Ask them to describe how it affected them and if there are any other harms they need to discuss
	3. Suggest an appropriate amend
	4. Ask them if this action is satisfactory or if they think additional actions are necessary.
Experience	Deep recognition and acceptance of the harmful impact of prior attitude and behavior. Healing and release of those harmed. Release from guilt and shame, and personal healing.
Result	Ability to walk into any room, remember any person or event, and feel resolved with all living and dead people ever encountered.
Promise	Freedom. Usefulness. Restored humanity.

Reflection Questions

1. Am I willing to change my attitude and behavior?

2. Am I willing to be changed in ways I'm unaware of and may not be able to control?

3. Am I willing to address each harm that I'm aware of, using the Step Nine amends process?

4. Am I being rigorously honest with myself and my sponsor/guide about the nature of each harm?

5. Do I hold myself accountable to a sponsor/guide for the preparation of each amend and the completion of all my amends?

6. Am I willing to complete all my amends using creative solutions for individuals I can't find or shouldn't see?

7. Is finishing my amends a top priority in my life?

8. Have I finished *all* my amends?

Meditation

Remember, underneath each step is powerlessness.

We are powerless:
- To be honest about the actual harm done to others.
- To accept responsibility for the damage we've caused.
- To tell the truth to ourselves, to our sponsor/guide, and the person harmed.
- To repair the damage done to others.
- To change our attitude and behavior.

Remember, we are on a journey: coming from, living in, evolving toward, Spirit. We are inherently flawed but deeply supported. We live and move and have our being in Spirit—the Source of Power.

We have been invited to a dance—a Cosmic dance. Grace has extended the invitation; Grace has given us the willingness; our willingness and our actions invite the continuous flow of Grace. It's all very mysterious. It's all very real.

What an adventure!

What a gift!

What a dance!

10

Step Ten

"Continued to take personal inventory and when we were wrong promptly admitted it."

Prayer

My consciousness is my responsibility.

Being awake is the key; taking action is the path.

Wisdom Spirit please allow me to:
See as You see—inclusively
Hear as You hear—undefended
Feel as You feel—compassionately
Think as You think—tolerantly
Act as You do—with loving kindness.

Reach out and touch me from the depth of Your divinity.

Allow me to be a channel *to* You for others.

Allow me to be a channel *from* You to others.

Please bring me to really believe:
The more I am emptied of false self, the more I am filled with
true Self
The more I embrace You, the more of the real me is present
The more I release others, the greater freedom I possess
The more of me I give away, the more of You I have.

Chapter Ten

Continue Emotional and Spiritual Growth

"The spiritual life is not a theory. *We have to live it.*" (BB page 83)

"We have entered the world of the Spirit." (BB page 84) So where have we been? In the world of self-will!

By now, alcohol is not the problem (first half of Step One)—unmanageability is (second half of Step One). We have a spiritual malady. Bill Wilson calls it a cancer of the soul. Our will is inherently defective; this is the human condition—self-will run riot.

The purpose of Steps One through Nine is deflation of the ego at depth. However, as Dr. Tiebout (psychiatrist who studied alcoholism and a good friend of Bill's) said, "The ego regenerates itself."

The 12 & 12 confirms a spiritual axiom: whenever we are disturbed, there is something wrong with us. It talks about Step Ten as a tool to be used as a spot-check inventory. Some confuse it with the Step Eleven nightly review; others suggest doing Step Ten in writing. Neither approach is suggested in the BB or the 12 & 12. Step Ten is a process to use immediately when we become awake to the fact that we are disturbed, that we've been spiritually asleep.

> Don't wait to write; don't wait for night.

The promises described at the end of Step Nine "... will always materialize if we work for them." (BB page 84) What is this work? We are asleep dreaming that we are awake.

The BB:

- Counsels us "... to watch ..." (page 84), to be awake, to stay conscious of ourselves, our attitudes, our motives, our feelings, our behavior. *This* is the work!
- Suggests that we vigorously begin "... this way of living as we cleaned up the past." (page 84) I believe this means that, when we begin making our Step Nine amends, we get instructions on and begin to do Steps Ten, Eleven, and Twelve.

My experience shows that Dr. Tiebout was right. I'm a human being and I constantly revert to old habits, previous reactions, and very non-spiritual behavior. Step Ten captures the Steps Four through Nine process—allowing us to identify and have removed the sludge produced daily by our self-will. Our goal is "... to grow in understanding and effectiveness." (BB page 84) Remember our model of the human being—the two components that make us human yet diminish our ability to be truly human:

- Our *mind* that allows us to know

- Our *will* that allows us to make decisions and to take actions.

> "We have a daily reprieve contingent on the maintenance of our spiritual condition." (BB page 85)
>
> Reprieve: stay of execution

The BB suggests using our *mind* to develop our vision of God's will, each day—our goal, purpose, and mission today. We have a responsibility to try to figure out, to actually know, what God wants of us today. Who does God want us to be; what does God want us to do? We are asking for and receiving direction. We seek guidance. Over time, we develop a vital sixth sense, an intuition, an inspiration.

The BB suggests that we also use our *will*—to align our will with God's. With this attitude, we cannot fail. Attitude—the position of the sail to allow it to catch the wind and give the ship power.

An ocean liner is regularly off course. But when the captain sets the automatic pilot for a predetermined destination, the homeostatic device in the ship that senses direction constantly corrects for the impact of the shift in currents and keeps the ship on course. Step Ten is our homeostatic device, keeping us lined up with our vision of God's will, correcting our course when we're pushed off target by selfishness and its primary manifestations: resentment, fear, and dishonesty.

Cynthia Bourgeault (*Wisdom of Jesus*) calls this mechanism our spiritual GPS: God Position System. Our new attitude allows us to see our deviations from the path, our mistakes—not as an accusation or judgment, but merely as a correctable event.

> How to discern what is God's will:
>
> - I'm in self-will when I experience:
>   - Resentment
>   - Fear
>   - Dishonesty (secrets)
>   - Selfishness
>
> - I'm in God's will when I experience:
>   - Loving kindness
>   - Trust (acceptance)
>   - Rigorous honesty (transparency)
>   - Altruism

Notice, none of these words is about comfort and happiness. Life is still difficult (Scott Peck). We still encounter speed bumps, but we now have adequate shock absorbers to smooth out the ride. We are, in reality, equipped with real tools.

We never become perfect, but we sure do make wonderful progress. Our life generally is happy, joyous, and free. We experience a sense of ease and comfort. We continue to become more awake, to feel a progressive shift (improvement) in our consciousness.

But happy, joyous, and free feelings, as well as the sense of ease and comfort, are by-products of right attitude, right thinking, and especially of right action.

We consistently lean into this way of life and become aware that the Spirit receives this leaning and draws us forward, moving us deeper into Spirit.

We have been taken to true freedom:

- There is no longer any significant conflict or struggle in acting in harmony with the Divine in us

- We are in conformity with the Divine outside of us (Nature)

- There is a correlation between our inner motives and our external behavior.

    - Paraphrased from *God For Us* by Catherine La Cugna

In the BB, we are asked to pray: "Thy will be done!" We are thus placed in harmony with the Universe. We are One with the energy that emanates from Source as reality unfolds; we are in the flow of the Stream of Life.

We have used our two human faculties properly:

- Our *mind,* to know God's will

- Our *will,* to freely choose to be in harmony with God's will.

We will continue to watch for:

- Selfishness
- Dishonesty
- Resentment
- Fear.

When (not **if** !) these crop up:

1. Ask God at once to remove them (because we're powerless over our character defects)

2. Discuss them with someone immediately (because we're given to self-deception)

3. Make amends quickly (to correct harm done)

4. Turn our thoughts resolutely to helping someone else (other-centeredness is the ultimate solution to the problem of self-centeredness).

We once again use the heart of the step process (Four through Nine) for restoring our inner tranquility and our outer relationships with those in our community. We are turned from a focus on self to a relationship with OTHER/others.

Our code is love and tolerance of others. This is an ideal, a vision. It is a process, not an event.

The channel of Grace in us is cleared. The Sunlight of the Spirit deep down inside us (BB page 55) is allowed to shine up and through us. It's like taking an inside shower. We are restored to sanity (BB page 37—sanity: ability for healthy, proportional thinking).

With respect to alcohol, we have been rendered completely neutral. No fight. No temptation. The problem has been removed. The only requirement is that we stay in fit spiritual condition.

There is a Native American story about a medicine man and his pupil, who complains that there appear to be two forces in conflict within himself—a white wolf and a black wolf. The medicine man agrees with this observation. The pupil asks: "Which one wins?" The medicine man replies: "The one you feed the most!"

Step Ten is a most practical tool for growth in emotional sobriety:

- Instead of resentment, we develop a heart given to forgiveness and an attitude of loving kindness

- Instead of fear, we trust God and manifest loving behavior toward, and compassion for, others

- Instead of dishonesty, we use honest self-appraisal and rigorous honesty with others; we foster the virtue of justice

- Instead of selfishness, we use self-restraint and manifest courtesy.

We learn to live undefended. We co-create our spiritual/emotional sobriety with acts contrary to our self-will.

We are not *cured* of our spiritual malady even when we have *recovered* from alcohol. We have a *daily* reprieve ... requiring the proper use daily of our mind and our will.

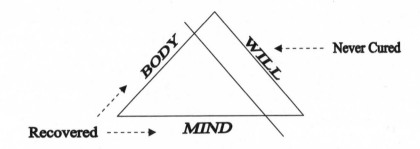

The first half of Step One is no longer an issue. Our experience of neutrality to alcohol (or our specific brokenness) is a Gift, a Grace. We are no longer possessed by the mental obsession and therefore the physical allergy is irrelevant. However, unmanageability is part of being human. And human power is powerless in healing this spiritual malady. So we pray.

When we are restored to our true humanity—made in the image and likeness of our Creator—we love ... and that overflows into service.

Summary

Purpose   Grow in wisdom and compassion by constantly being re-aligned to our vision of God's Will

Instructions   1. Read, hightlight and outline BB pages 84 and 85
2. Read Step Ten in the 12 & 12, then supplement the BB outline above.

Process   When disturbed by selfishness (as manifest in resentment, fear, and dishonesty), use:
1. Prayer
2. Confession
3. Amends
4. Service.

Experience   After awareness of being disturbed, restoration to inner peace and reintegration into reality.

Result   Expand self-consciousness; improve God-consciousness; manifest service-consciousness.

Promise   Growth in understanding and effectiveness.

Reflection Questions

1. Am I committed to a daily effort to grow in understanding and effectiveness? What does this mean for me—practically?

2. Am I willing to improve my consciousness? To be truly awake? To watch for deviations from my commitment to the spiritual path?

3. Am I willing to hold myself accountable to another human being when I become aware that I am disturbed?

4. Am I compassionate with myself for my failures and do I really trust in God's Grace for my improvement?

5. Am I willing to continue to make amends when I'm aware of any new harm I've caused any other human being?

6. Do I attempt to consciously practice the behaviors contrary to those emanating from my character defects: the virtues of loving kindness, trust (acceptance), rigorous honesty (transparency), and altruism?

Meditation

Above all, trust in the slow work of God. We are, quite naturally, impatient in everything to reach the end without delay.

We would like to skip the intermediate stages. We are impatient with being on the way to something unknown, something new, and yet it is the law of progress that it is made by passing through stages of instability—and that may take a very long time.

And so it is with us. Our ideas and values mature gradually — let them grow, let them shape themselves without undue haste. Don't try to force them on, as though we could be today what time (Grace and circumstances and acting on our own good will) will make us tomorrow.

Only God could say what this new spirit, gradually forming within us, will be. Give God the benefit of believing that God's hand is leading us and accept the anxiety of feeling ourselves in suspense and incomplete.

- Adaptation of a reading from Pierre de Chardin

11

Step Eleven

"Sought through prayer and meditation to improve our conscious contact with God, *as we understood Him*, praying only for knowledge of His will for us and the power to carry that out."

Prayer

"My Lord God, I have no idea where I am going. I do not see the road ahead of me. I cannot know for certain where it will end. Nor do I really know myself, and the fact that I think I am following Your will does not mean I am actually doing so. But I believe that the desire to please You does in fact please You. And I hope I have that desire in all I am doing. I hope I will never do anything apart from that desire. And I know if I do this You will lead me by the right road though I may know nothing about it. Therefore will I trust You always though I may seem to be lost and in the shadow of death. I will not fear, for You are ever with me, and You will never leave me to face my perils alone."

- Thomas Merton. *Thoughts in Solitude*

Chapter Eleven

Improve Our Conscious Contact With Power: Prayer and
Meditation

In Step One we saw from our own experience that our
unenlightened mind does not receive or process information
correctly and that our uninformed (un-Graced) will does not
decide or implement effectively. In Step Two we made a
decision that we are in *constant* contact (Immanence and
Transcendence). We made a decision to name God. In Step
Three we made a decision to have a relationship and to
surrender to God (to be informed and conformed).

Steps Four through Nine are tools that cleaned out the
sludge in the channel to allow Grace to flow freely and
effectively in and through us.

Step Ten is intended to keep the channel open and clear.

Step Eleven's mission is "to improve our conscious
contact" ... to inform our *mind* with "knowledge of His will"
and to infuse our *will* with "the power to carry that out."

> In Step Two, we realize *constant* contact. In
> Step Eleven, we attempt to improve *conscious*
> contact.

As the result of consistently practicing prayer and
meditation we are brought to *constant consciousness*.

"... this awareness of a Power greater than ourselves is the essence of spiritual experience. Our more religious members call it God-consciousness." (BB page 570: Appendix II)

The nature of our disease is "Selfishness—self-centeredness!" (BB page 62) The nature of the antidote is OTHER/other-centeredness. We must be turned from this natural state of self-focus to a spiritual state of focus on OTHER/other. Notice the language: we must *be* turned. This differentiates the Twelve-Step process from self-help. We cannot do this. It must be done to us—not by us. We submit to a process. We do lots of work. This demonstrates our willingness to have our willfulness set aside. But it is Grace that does the setting aside, the change, the conversion, the transformation.

The spiritual life is like a coin having two sides: one side is a relationship with OTHER; the other side is a relationship with others (Steps Eleven and Twelve, respectively).

Spiritual Coin

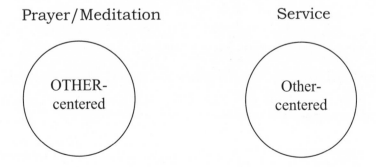

Prayer/Meditation — OTHER-centered

Service — Other-centered

> BB Chapter 7 (Working with Others) begins
> "Practical experience shows that nothing will
> so much insure immunity from drinking as
> intensive work with other alcoholics." (page 89)
> This indicates service protects, while
> prayer/meditation heals.

In reviewing the major religious traditions I see two fundamental operating principles:

1. Love God with all your mind, with all your heart, with all your strength;

2. Love your neighbor as yourself (or as God loves you).

Twelve-Step spirituality distills from the experience of the Christian tradition (through the Oxford Group) these two principles in Steps Eleven and Twelve.

In Bill's story it says at the top of BB page 14, that this program is "Simple but not easy; a price has to be paid. It meant destruction of self-centeredness. I must turn in all things to the Father of Light who presides over us all." This states the importance of Step Eleven.

And at the bottom of this same page: "For if an alcoholic failed to perfect and enlarge his spiritual life through work and self-sacrifice for others, he could not survive the certain trials and low spots ahead. If he did not work, he would surely drink again, and if he drank, he would surely die." This states the importance of Step Twelve.

Before his death in 1950, Dr. Bob Smith said to Bill Wilson: "Let's keep it simple—love and service" (Steps Eleven and Twelve).

> "Stillness is what creates Love.
>
> Movement is what creates Life.
>
> To be still yet still moving—that is everything."
>
> –Do Hyun Choe, Sugi Master

By this time in the process (having finished or in the midst of making Step Nine amends) the alcohol problem has usually been removed, yet we retain the spiritual "cancer of the soul." Perhaps we could look at prayer and meditation as the intervention of chemotherapy and radiation—to restore and heal the soul. Daily, they give us a vision of God's will (knowledge) and the means to effect it (Power). They place us in harmony with the Universe as God manifests moment to moment to moment.

In the 12 & 12, Bill comments in Step Eleven that just as air, food, water, and sunshine are vital (Latin word "*vita*" means "life") for the body, prayer and meditation are necessary for the soul. Perhaps prayer and meditation are our medication for the spiritual malady ... our daily prescription to bring us to God-reliance, rather than self-reliance.

Many people have a problem being consistent with prayer and meditation (even those who know how important it is).

They think they don't have the time, don't know how, or don't get results—then they give up after a short period of effort.

To practice Step Eleven regularly, it must be seen as a value—a real necessity (not a mandate, or another "should"). This comes from:

- A deep personal experience of Step One—personal powerlessness and a desperate conviction of the need for Power

- A firm, clear decision in Step Two about who God is, where God is, and the true nature of faith.

After years of study and experience, I can honestly say that the BB instructions on prayer and meditation (pages 85–88) are the simplest, yet most effective, that I have encountered. They form the basic structure of my daily practice. Bill Wilson is clear in these instructions that we should consult with professionals (minister, rabbi, priest) and read other books on the subject. I have done that to put flesh on the bones of the basic structure I developed from the combination of the BB and the 12 & 12.

> Prayer and meditation. Two words; two processes.

Prayer is when we are talking to God; meditation is when we are listening to God.

We pray not to change God, but to be changed. Through prayer (intimate conversation with a trusted friend) we become conscious and demonstrate a willingness and openness to be changed.

There are many types/purposes of prayer:

- Petition   recognition of our God-reliance
- Repentance   recognition of forgiveness
- Thanksgiving   recognition of gratitude
- Praise   recognition of Mystery

A 1934 dictionary defined the word "meditation" as "directed thinking."

The BB (page 86) suggests that "on awakening ... we ask (petition) God to direct our thinking." "We ask God" is a BB code that means we pray. It's this simple: God, please direct my thinking.

The man who took me through the step work in 1988 said we ask for our thinking to be directed, then we begin thinking, and trust that the thoughts that come are God-inspired.

".. we can employ our mental faculties with assurance, for after all God gave us brains to use." (BB page 86) Once we have completed the first nine Steps, this is a relatively safe direction, for our minds have been restored to sanity, the sludge in us has been identified and cleared, and we are on a path of God-reliance (though regularly disturbed by our deviations toward self-reliance).

This is where the listening comes in—we listen to our thinking. God does not speak to most people audibly. But centuries of wisdom and experience counsel us to listen to the small voice of inspiration. The BB further instructs:

- Think about the 24 hours ahead. What are you going to *do* today? Scan your day as if reviewing a day-timer or pocket calendar. Are your activities in harmony with your vision of God's will for you today?

- Consider your plans for the day. Who are you going to *be* today? Listen for a word or phrase: today, be honest, be patient, be mindful, be helpful—your theme for the day. Often this will be an antidote to the character defect du jour.

If on a given morning you're distracted or fidgety, some reading may energize and focus you. I like to choose a short selection from one of many spiritual books I keep available. Step Eleven in the 12 & 12 suggests a prayer such as the Prayer of St. Francis. A method with a long history in the Christian tradition is known as "*Lectio Divina*" or divine reading, where you read a word or phrase and reflect on its meaning, context, application to your life, and possible invitation or challenge that it extends to you today.

Several years ago I expanded my practice to include a conscious, contemplative component (based on Thomas Keating's "Open Mind, Open Heart"). So, once I've concluded the thinking phase, I get quiet and try to be present to the Presence. I listen for the subtle whisper of the Soul of the Kosmos, that "unsuspected inner resource" (BB pages 569–

570), that "... Great Reality deep down within us" (BB page 55), the "... Creative Intelligence, a Spirit of the Universe underlying the totality of things ..." (BB page 46).

> Ken Wilber (*A Theory of Everything*) defines Kosmos as including all of reality, vs. cosmos, meaning the known universe.

I pray for an open heart—a special exercise of yearning for contact, longing for union. By definition, my mind (finite) cannot encompass or comprehend God (infinite); however, my heart (will) can reach out and embrace it. I sit in this Presence to absorb and be absorbed. I sit in this Presence with full *attention* of my mind, being aware but focused on a specific *intention* of my will being Loved and Loving. I notice God noticing me.

AA's long form of Tradition Twelve ends, we "... live in thankful contemplation of Him who presides over us all." (BB page 568) I lean into my intention; I stay gently pressed up against Spirit; and Spirit embraces me and moves me forward.

Several years ago I learned it's important to have consistency, some routine for this spiritual practice. I set a timer to avoid being distracted by wondering about the time. I commit to the time available for this particular morning (I originally started with 5 minutes and gradually worked it up to a minimum of 20). I have a specific place set up to support my practice: a chair, sitting pillow, timer, symbols from various traditions to remind/inspire me, books, Tibetan singing bowl, etc.

When the timer tells me my meditation period is concluded I finish with a set of prayers asking for knowledge, Power, freedom, Love, and opportunity to be of service. My final prayer is Step Seven. The last phrase of that prayer is such an appropriate launching for the day's activities "... as I go out from here, to do Your bidding." (BB page 76)

The BB actually begins its Step Eleven instruction with a series of questions to be asked "when we retire at night ..." It is another inventory—more soul surgery. It allows us, at the end of the day, to pick up issues not addressed during the day by Step Ten. Perhaps this instruction is placed first in the BB to set us up for the next morning's prayer and meditation practice. The final nighttime suggestion is to "... inquire (of God) what corrective measures should be taken." (BB page 98) The instructions suggest inventory not only of our deficiencies of the day, but also of our contributions. And it suggests that we do this review "constructively" not judgmentally. It cautions us to "... be careful not to drift into worry, remorse, or morbid reflections ..." And this suggestion is made not because it might make us feel bad, but because "... that would diminish our usefulness to others." This is the recurring theme of the recovery process, the spiritual path. Our life is not about ourselves. It is about our relationship with God and our helpfulness to others. Our personal happiness and peace of mind will not be found by looking for them. They will be by-products of pursuing our true purpose—to be of maximum service to God and the people about us. Some call this an examination of conscience; I like the phrase "examination of consciousness".

I conclude my evening prayer and meditation practice with a reflective praying of the Prayer of St. Francis—the prayer of transformation, the prayer of being turned from self to OTHER/others.

The BB concludes its Step Eleven instruction by suggesting that when we're agitated or doubtful, we pause and ask for the right thought or action. This dovetails nicely with Step Ten (to be used any time we are disturbed). The perfect prayer is recommended: "Thy will be done!" This is an act of my free will, placing me in harmony with the Universe: I will that Your will be done. This is the proper use of the will—a change from willfulness to willingness. We are thus singing one song: Uni-verse.

Appendix G contains an outline of my personal prayer and meditation practice (evening; morning; all day). I usually begin on my knees with the set-aside prayer. God doesn't care if I'm standing, sitting, or on my knees. I don't kneel to get God's attention; I kneel to get my attention. It is a symbol of my surrender, my subordination to a Power greater than myself. It is an attempt to behave humbly so that, maybe, I'll begin to think, feel, act, and actually be humble. Just maybe I'll seek and embrace humility.

I ask myself why I'm here doing this meditation. I try to become as conscious as possible, to be awake, alert, present. I repeat Step Eleven verbatim and focus on the mission statement "... to improve my conscious contact ..."

Then I sit:

- Back straight
- Eyes closed
- Feet on the floor if in a chair; cross-legged if on a meditation pillow
- Hands in lap
- Breathing: slow, deep, deliberate, gentle, rhythmic
- Body relaxed and comfortable
- Mind open, undefended, and attentive (acknowledging Presence)
- Heart (will) open, loving, and with intention (consenting to God's invitation to improved awareness).

We don't meditate to become good meditators; we meditate to improve our conscious contact with God ("I Ask For Wonder," Rabbi Heschel.)

Meditation is not a method. It is an attitude ... of being:

- Patient
- Expectant
- Compassionate, especially toward yourself
- Grateful
- Forgiving
- Inviting
- Welcoming
- Present to the moment: awake
- Present to Presence: yearning.

What distinguishes AA's Step Eleven from other forms of meditation is that it is about thinking, not about an empty mind or no thought. It is about listening to our thinking, after we pray for it to be directed by the Spirit.

We listen deeply to our thinking to hear and get guidance from that small voice, that subtle inspiration. Inevitably there will be distractions:

- Don't resist or reject them
- Neither cling to nor detach from them
- Let them flow like debris in a moving river
- Observe but don't engage them
- Remember the mission: to improve *conscious* contact
- Use a sacred word (mantra) to:
    - Return to your center (body)
    - Refocus your attention (mind)
    - Renew your intention (will)
    - Bring you back to awareness of Presence (consciousness)
    - Remind you of wonder and gratitude (attitude).

We attempt to detach from self and the world, to attach to Self and the Kosmos. We surrender. We are surrendered.

Meditation itself takes us into the threshold of Presence, a space of Grace. The process as outlined in the Big Book disciplines us—gives us structure and guidelines.

We pray not to change God's will, but to know it and to be changed—so that God's will and our will are one. We meditate to invite the Spirit of the Universe to open our minds and hearts to discover God's plan for us and to acquire the power to cooperate with and conform to that plan. Through this process we are hoping for and in pursuit of freedom from the bondage of self.

When I first did this work of the BB Steps in 1988 I realized, at depth, that I was thoroughly powerless and that my only hope for a quality sober life was contingent on establishing and maintaining an effective, personal relationship with a Power other than myself. I committed to a daily, consistent Step Eleven. I outlined it, developed a practice, had a sacred space, and sat every day for 15 minutes. For a whole year, I was convinced it had been a waste of time. My meditation period was plagued with distractions; I had few spiritual thoughts of any depth and very little awareness/feeling of the presence of God.

At the end of that year I suspected there was something wrong. I discussed my concern with some people in AA—they were not much help. I went to a priest—he was less help. He talked about the possibility of the Dark Night of the Soul. Well, that appealed to my ego, since it is a sign the 16th century mystic John of the Cross thought indicated advanced spiritual development. But I intuitively knew it was not my situation.

So I contacted a man who is not in any Twelve-Step program and is not ordained in institutional religion, but is very knowledgeable about the spiritual path. He had been a Trappist monk and had been mentored for six years by Thomas Merton. Jim Finley is now a clinical psychologist, spiritual director, and author.

I made an appointment and acquainted him with the Twelve-Step process (especially my experience of power-lessness and the absolute need for Power) as well as my meditation practice and frustrations.

After about 45 minutes of my talking, he responded. He observed that I was very task oriented, that I had structured a practice, sat consistently every day, and was attempting to will my own spiritual development as if it were a self-help project.

He commented that the spiritual life is a path of willingness, not willfulness. He suggested that I think of my relationship with my spiritual path in the same way that I think of my relationship with alcohol—that I am powerless over it. He also indicated that I think of my relationship to prayer and meditation in the same way—that I am powerless over them. Thus, he recommended that I come to prayer and meditation with the humble attitude of powerlessness and sit awake to the Presence of Power, ready to be taken to a place I don't even know exists.

He confirmed my job was to show up and make the effort. The results are none of my business.

What a relief! The cement overcoat of responsibility for results was removed. I've not had a problem with this since.

He phrased it this way:

> All people on a spiritual path have a spiritual practice, and
> they practice their practice, and
> they are faithful to their practice, and
> then their practice is faithful to them.

It is your *effort* that's important.

There is the story of the Buddhist novice who wanted to be enlightened. Everywhere the master went the novice followed, always asking for enlightenment. One day when on the shore of a lake, the master beckoned the novice to enter the lake. "Finally," the novice thought, "I'm going to be taken to a place of enlightenment." Both the master and the novice waded out until they were waist deep in the water. The master gently grasped the novice by the back of the neck and bent him forward until his head was under water. The novice was delighted at the thought that this was it! However, the master continued to hold the novice's head under water for a long, long time. The novice began to struggle—he was running out of air. Finally the master brought the novice to the surface, gasping for breath. "What are you doing?" the novice shouted. "When you want enlightenment as desperately as you just wanted air, you will find it."

With a twinkle in his eyes, Jim suggested that if I wanted to know whether my meditation was effective, I should ask my wife how I'm treating her! I will know the effectiveness of my meditation practice not by how I think or feel, but how I act.

I like the analogy of the battery-driven golf cart. All day long its job is to deliver golfers about the course. At night, it is hooked up to a battery charger to restore power. Without that, it would be useless the next day to fulfill its purpose. It sits in the presence of power, passively absorbing power.

My favorite sayings relating to prayer and meditation follow:

- Thomas Merton (*New Seeds of Contemplation*)— meditation is the combustion chamber of the ego; a place where the false self is dismantled.

- Thomas Keating (*Open Mind, Open Heart*)— deep contemplation has a therapeutic healing effect, releasing the darkness of the false self stored in our cellular structure, bringing it into the healing presence of the Divine Therapist.

- Ron Rolheiser (*Holy Longing*)— through meditation we are absorbed into the fire that is God; to be consumed and become One with God.

- Hildegard of Bingen (12th century mystic)— between me and God there is no between.

- Augustine of Hippo (4th century Christian theologian):
  - God is closer to me than I am to myself.
  - My heart is made for You; I cannot rest until I rest in You.

- Meister Eckert (13th century mystic)—God is closer to me than the air I breathe.

- Peace Pilgrim (biography)— there is nowhere there is not God.

- St. Paul (1st century Christian)— in God I live, and move, and have my being.

- Thomas Keating (*Intimacy With God*):

- The world is a magnet that draws us away from our Center

- God is the real center of gravity, inviting us inward

- Contemplation is a radical consenting to the inner force; when we let go (surrender) we are brought to intimacy with this Energy

- My mind is responsible for my attention; my will (heart) is responsible for my intention

- My mind allows me awareness of God's Presence; my will places me in consent to the action of God in me.

- Jim Finley (*Christian Meditation*):

  - Let God have His way with us

  - I am willing, but Grace does the work. My practice fosters the subtle impulse to Love and be Loved.

- Thomas Merton— Humans have an unquenchable cosmic thirst that can only be quenched through union with God.

- Gabriel Marcel— Light illumines the darkness. But we do not usually see the aperture through which it shines.

- Anonymous— We must pray as if everything depends on God, and work as if everything depends on us. (Maybe it is more true that we must pray as if everything depends on us, and work as if everything depends on God.)

This relationship of will and God's Grace is a cosmic dance—the divine alchemy that produces transformation. Over time, I am changed in the way I think, the way I feel, and especially the way I behave. And it's done to me, not by me. I must make the effort; the results are disproportionate to that effort. This is enlightenment—the ability to discern between reality and my human illusions and delusions.

> Our concept of God is the very thing that may prevent our relationship with God!

Remember your Step Two decision: God *is*!

Remember the Step Two promises:

- "... we had to search fearlessly ... think honestly ... search diligently within yourself ..." then "... you can join us on the Broad Highway ..." and "With this attitude you cannot fail." (BB page 55)

- "... He has come to all who have honestly sought Him. When we drew near to Him, He disclosed Himself to us!" (BB page 57)

Remember your Step Three decision: to have a relationship with your Higher Power.

Remember the Step Three promises, especially: God will provide what I need.

In meditation we leave everything behind for Love's sake. Our cherished delusions about our self must die. In a contemplative retreat, Jim Finley shared that our actual death is the exhale of our final breath, responding to the simultaneous inhale of God's breath such that we are drawn to union with God—as a needle is brought to a magnet. This is indeed a dying of self to be reborn in Self. Eckert Tolle, in his book "Power of Now," suggests that the secret to life is to die before we die and realize there is no death.

The Prayer of St. Francis concludes: "It is by dying that one awakens to eternal life."   (see Appendix G)

Summary

Purpose	Improve conscious contact with God, as we understand Him.
Instructions	Read and highlight: 1. BB pages 85–88 2. Step Eleven in the 12 & 12. Outline the BB material to create a personal practice.
Process	Begin a consistent daily prayer and meditation practice.
Experience	Taking responsibility for the effort; the results are up to God and are none of our business.
Result	Improve *conscious* contact; a gradual change in the way we think, feel, and behave.
Promise	Inspiration (intuition) will become a working part of the mind. We come to rely upon it. God will discipline us in this simple way. We will sense the flow of the Spirit in us. We will develop a vital sixth sense.

* * * * *

Remember: progress, **not** perfection!

Reflection Questions

1. What do I really believe about God? Who God is? Where God is? What is God's impact on my life?

2. Do I believe prayer and meditation are really necessary? Does my life depend on them?

3. How do I come to value prayer and meditation as priorities in my daily schedule?

4. What do I need to do specifically to become more competent in prayer and meditation?

5. How can I distinguish between what is God's will and what is my self-will?

6. How can I tell the difference between willingness and willfulness?

7. Do I really want Divine guidance? Do I believe it is available? Do I listen for it? Do I respond to it?

8. What is preventing me from having a regular prayer and meditation practice?

Meditation

We have entered the world of the Spirit—we do this by exiting the world of self.
The spiritual life is not a theory—we have to live it.

We have a daily reprieve (from the spiritual malady) contingent on the maintenance of our spiritual condition.

Every day we must seek God's will:
- To know it
- To do it.

We are to grow in understanding and effectiveness.

The mission of Step Eleven is to receive:
- Knowledge of God's will
- Power to be in harmony with God's will.

We don't pray and meditate to change God's will;
we pray and meditate to *know* God's will, to be changed.

We don't pray and meditate to become good meditators, but to improve our *conscious* contact.

We approach God for in – spiration, to breathe Spirit into us.

We sit in God's Presence; being absorbed into the Spirit and absorbing the Spirit.

Thus, are we transformed!

(con't)

God cannot change (by definition); this means:

- God cannot Love me more; no matter what I do or don't do.
- God cannot Love me less; no matter what I do or don't do.
- God Loves me unconditionally (there are no conditions because God doesn't need anything or anybody).

12

Step Twelve

"Having had a spiritual awakening as the result of these steps, we tried to carry this message to alcoholics, and to practice these principles in all our affairs."

Prayer

Holy Spirit—open up our hearts to appreciate the gifts we have received:
- We've been given life—we get to experience this adventure of living
- We've been given freedom—we live in a country built on respect for the rights of individuals
- We've been given education—we have the resources to become as informed as we want to be
- We've been given recovery—we have a path that leads to physical, emotional, and spiritual sobriety
- We've been given love—we have the opportunity to experience being Loved and the opportunity of expressing Love
- We've been given a vision—we are invited to be in harmony with the Spirit of the Universe
- We've been given purpose—we may live in conscious contact with the Mystery at the foundation of reality; to serve in constant consciousness of the manifestation of Mystery through helping those around us   (con't)

- We've been given community—we have a Fellowship that thrives on helping one another.

Holy Spirit of the Universe—thank You for Your generosity!

Allow me to hear Your invitation. Empower me to respond in loving service. Allow me to be generous.

Chapter Twelve

Enlarge Our Personal Spiritual Life: Service

> "A small group of awakened people can change the world. Indeed, it is the only thing that ever has."
>
> –Margaret Mead

We drink the water of the world to satisfy our thirst, and it only creates more thirst—unquenchable. We drink in meditation from the Source, the Wellspring of Life. This water of the Spirit we sip in prayer and meditation is gradually absorbed by our soul and creates our own deep spring which eventually and inevitably overflows for others to drink. This new well can never be emptied as long as it's used to keep filling others' cups. This is the sacrament of service—the outward behavior that creates and maintains the inward reality.

We are asleep, dreaming that we are awake!

The promise of the Twelve-Step process is one of a "spiritual awakening." The only change in the Twelve Steps since the first BB printing in 1939 was in Step Twelve, in the First Edition, second printing. The first printing used the term spiritual "experience"; all subsequent printings contain the phrase spiritual "awakening." Appendix II was included in the second printing to explain that "experience" connotes a sudden change; "awakening" suggests a gradual change. The result of both an experience and an awakening is a change. We are changed in the way we think, the way we feel, and especially in the way we behave. And, again, what distinguishes the Twelve-Step process from self-help programs is that this change is done *to* us, not *by* us.

The person having an *experience* will be very aware of it as it is happening; the person being *awakened* may be totally unconscious and unaware that any change whatsoever is taking place. Spiritual experience is like a light switch (on/off); spiritual awakening is like a dimmer switch (gradual—one click at a time). Most spiritual transformations are of the spiritual awakening variety.

In the previous chapter I described the spiritual life as a coin having two sides:

- One side a relationship with OTHER (Higher Power)

- The other side, service to others (humanity).

This is a wonderful symbolic image to help us interpret reality; to help us understand who we are, and what we are, and how we are to live. It is not an imposition on us to be of service. It is how we are built. It is our very nature. It is our purpose. It is our destiny.

> To know and love God;

> To love and serve one another.

God is Love and Love is a verb. Of its very nature, by definition, Love is action. Although God is all Powerful, in one respect God is powerless. God *must* create. God, by God's own very nature, must be generative, must overflow God's own Self. The world, the things in it, and especially humans are the necessary result of this overflow of God's Self.

Hebrew scripture describes creation of humans by God breathing into the mud and making us in God's own image and likeness—making us male and female.

Image = having the ability to know; *likeness* = having the ability to make a decision, to act, to create.

Evolution of Spiritual AWAKENING:

self happens

shit happens

sit happens

shift happens

Spirit happens

Self happens!

Dr. Bob Smith, cofounder of AA, in his last talk summed up our way of life in the words: "love and service."

The BB (page 35) relates Jim's story about the man who puts a little whiskey in his milk. There is a suggestion as to the cause of his relapse: "... he failed to enlarge his spiritual life ..." (BB page 35) At first glance, I interpreted that to mean Jim had not made enough effort to have a relationship with God through prayer and meditation. However, when I was directed to the bottom of BB page 14, I saw this phrase again, but in a different context. "For if an alcoholic failed to perfect and enlarge his spiritual life through work and self-sacrifice for others ..." We are encouraged to seek a personal spiritual life empowered by a consistent practice of Step Eleven. However, we enlarge that spiritual life through self-sacrificial service for others. While recently listening to a tape of Bill Wilson's talk at the Long Beach, California convention in 1960, I heard him say through Step Twelve "we perfect our conscious contact with God." The spiritual coin.

There is a natural progression of turning us inside out, from a life-taking habit of self-obsession to a life-giving desire for service to others. It grows from the inside rather than being imposed from the outside. Organic!

Spiritual transformation is authentic conversion. A deep desire to help begins to emerge. A true compassion for the suffering of others grows slowly but inevitably. The more my actions respond to this energy, the more I see the impact on peoples' lives. And this becomes a generative, dynamic cycle nurtured by my consistent practice of prayer and meditation. The Spirit invites me to more self-emptying and yet continually supplies the well to overflowing.

First we "must" do service as a conscious willingness— acts contrary to our will (perhaps even reluctant robotic response to sponsor direction). This begins to re-form our psychology (and even our biology—see Dr. Daniel Siegel's "mindsight" research at UCLA School of Psychiatry) to a new way of thinking, feeling and then a new way of behaving.

"... nothing will so much insure immunity from drinking as intensive work with other alcoholics." (BB page 89) Immunization! That's the healing serum we are given when we turn our thoughts and actions to being of service, to really helping others.

Inevitably for those who have an authentic spiritual awakening (and a reliable sign of it) we "must" manifest in service as the very nature of our transformed self. After we are awakened, placed in harmony with Source, re-integrated and in union with our Creator, we become like God. We are like a spring that bubbles naturally to the surface, or an oil well drilled to a reservoir that spouts wildly upward.

We become a source of solace and service to our community. It is no longer the "must" of duty imposed from the outside; it is the "must" of our very nature, an energy generated from the inside.

This is one of those spiritual paradoxes: the more I serve others, the more my life is taken care of. The more I am emptied of false self, the more I am restored to true Self. The more of me I give away, the more of me I have.

> Bill Wilson is very clear in the BB (page 130) that we live with our head in the clouds (Step Eleven) but we keep our feet firmly planted on earth (Step Twelve).

Our problem is three-fold; the complete program of recovery is represented by the triangle:

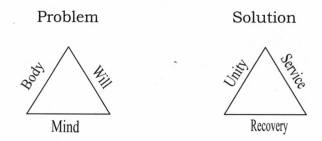

Problem   Solution

Body / Will / Mind   Unity / Service / Recovery

Each part of the program has 12 principles:

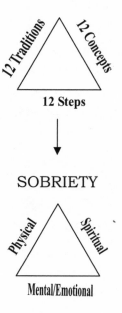

12 Traditions / 12 Concepts / 12 Steps

SOBRIETY

Physical / Spiritual / Mental/Emotional

Faith without works is dead (from the letter of James in the Christian scripture). However, works without faith is a formula for burnout. And indeed, faith without action is fantasy.

Our task is to stay gently pressed up against our way of life. We lean into Spirit. We take the next indicated action, especially acts contrary to our will. We allow Spirit to lead us. We maintain an attitude of gratitude and compassion, not only compassionate action for others, but especially compassion for ourselves in humble recognition of our humanity.

Chuck C. ("New Pair of Glasses") captures the principle of recovery (other-centeredness) when he suggests an attitude toward our families, our coworkers, our customers, and our world in general: "How can I help you get done what you need to get done?" And he suggests we do it for fun and for free.

Let's pause here and get a real practical perspective from our experience. How do we get and stay sober?

By not drinking?	No: detox facilities, jails, hospitals, and asylums have a dismal record
By going to meetings?	No: Bill and Bob had none
Through sponsorship?	No: Ebby (Bill's sponsor) got drunk; Bob (sponsored by Bill) got drunk

By knowledge of the BB?	No: Bill and Bob and the first 100 didn't have one
By the Twelve Steps?	No: for the first four years there were none (except the Oxford Group's six steps)
Through a spiritual experience?	No: Bob did not have one (he experienced a slow spiritual awakening)
Through prayer and meditation?	No: Bob and Anne prayed and meditated every day while they were members of the Oxford Group for 2-1/2 years before they met Bill (Bob got drunk after every meeting!)
Through discussion about God?	No: Bill, Anne, and Bob had daily discussions and Bob got drunk after his first period of sobriety.

Let's take a look at Bill's actual experience.

Before leaving for Akron in 1935, Bill, sober six months, was complaining to Lois that his efforts with alcoholics were not working. Despite a concerted, daily reaching out to alcoholics, he had failed to get anybody sober. He speculated that perhaps he had misinterpreted his spiritual experience and should go back to Wall Street to resume being a stock broker.

Lois looked at him and exclaimed: *"You* are sober." Bill got it. His effort was what counted, not his results. This is what he remembered when, in Akron late one Friday afternoon, broke and discouraged, he was tempted to go into the bar at the Mayflower Hotel, but instead reached out to find a drunk to help.

After meeting Bill, Bob got sober. For the first time he realized that it wasn't a moral issue of willpower, but that he was physically and mentally powerless. That knowledge, and the efforts of Anne and Bill in prayer and meditation, plus the daily presence of and discussions with Bill, still didn't keep him sober. Only after completing his amends and then joining Bill in calling on drunks in asylums (Jim: BB pages 35–37) and hospitals (Fred: BB pages 39–43; Bill D. page xvii), did Bob stay sober until his death in 1950.

This process is counter-intuitive. Our culture and common wisdom say we must know better and then feel better before we can do better. The experience of Twelve-Step recovery suggests the opposite is true. We need to do better in order to feel better and then we'll know better. The BB confirms this on page 64:

> "... we have been not only mentally and physically ill, we have been spiritually sick. When the spiritual malady is overcome, we straighten out mentally and physically."

So how do we get and stay sober?

The BB confirms it's by carrying the message to others:

Page xxii: Bill's experience, simple and personal—"...
               recovery begins when one alcoholic talks to
               another alcoholic, sharing experience,
               strength, and hope."

Page xvi: Bob's experience—"One alcoholic could affect
               another as no non-alcoholic could. It also
               indicated that strenuous work, one alcoholic
               with another, was vital to permanent
               recovery."

Page 20:   Accumulated experience—"Our very lives as
               ex-problem drinkers depend upon our
               constant thought of others and how we might
               meet their needs."

Actions contrary to the will! We have been taken out of
the world of self (self-will, willfulness). We have entered the
World of the Spirit (God's will, willingness).

> Clancy I. (Los Angeles) says that action is the
> magic word. The formula is one drunk talking to
> another, reducing the feelings of difference, to
> allow them to take actions they don't believe in.

The BB refers to Step Twelve as the "... foundation stone of your recovery. A kindly act once in a while isn't enough. You have to act the Good Samaritan every day, if need be." (page 97)

Step Twelve also includes "... practicing these principles in all our affairs." Thus the BB chapters following Chapter 7 "Working With Others" are included in the Step Twelve instructions:

Chapter 8   To Wives (our significant relationship)

Chapter 9   The Family Afterwards (our families)

Chapter 10   To Employers (our work)

Chapter 11   A Vision for You (our community).

This material (Chapters 7 through 11) comprises 41% of the BB (counting all Roman numerals through page 164).

Thus, Step One (34%) and Step Twelve (41%) represent 75% of the instructions on how to get and stay sober, on how to enter, then maintain, a spiritual way of life.

In the fear inventory of Step Four we are challenged to identify our role in the world: what are we to do; who are we to be? (page 68). Perhaps the BB answers this question: "Your job now is to be at the place where you may be of maximum helpfulness to others ..." (page 102)

The 12 & 12 comments that the joy of living is the theme of Step Twelve and action is its key word. Right action is the key to good living.

We don't think or feel our way into right action. We take the right actions, then healthy thinking and good feelings will follow.

But this is not always convenient, comfortable, or easy. The BB uses the terms "... work and self-sacrifice ..." (page 15). Sacrifice! This word comes from two Latin words:

- Sacer—to be holy, priestly

- Facere—to make, create.

This service to others, through sacrifice of our self, is sacred work: it heals others and at the same time it heals us.

Going to hospitals, jails, asylums, etc., is still very effective and necessary service. However, today people suffering various forms of addiction populate Twelve-Step meetings. In these meetings we can witness to the message by our presence and sometimes by our words. Meetings are like emergency rooms for the mentally and spiritually ill and the terminally wounded. It's fine to go there for Fellowship and inspiration, but far better to attend meetings to see how we can help. As Bill Wilson said, sometimes the good is the enemy of the best.

Check your motives for attending meetings and then go anyway. Try to reach out to help someone, anyone. Ultimately, it nourishes your soul. Meetings are a place where the weak can get strong and the strong can feel safe with their weakness. Richard Rohr says that our willingness to be used leads to healing—ours and theirs.

Whole-e-ness is contagious. An open and generous smile invites (and even pulls) others into the flow of the Universe.

Neils Bohr (astrophysicist) speculates that we live in a force field whether we're aware of it or not. Our job is to become conscious of it and to channel the available Power to those around us.

> Churchill said we make a living by what we get, but we make a life by what we give.

Service is any altruistic action we take that promotes or supports recovery/healing of someone else. There are lots of opportunities to be helpful:

- setting up/breaking down meetings
- coffee commitment
- literature person
- secretary/chairperson/treasurer
- greeting/welcoming
- General Service Representative (GSR), Central Service Representative (CSR)
- Grapevine representative
- hospitals and institutions
- time keeper to monitor sharing
- providing information to non-alcoholic groups
- speaking
- attending meetings to witness to recovery.

Then there is the more direct work of one-on-one sponsorship and/or helping someone go through the process of applying the Twelve Steps to their personal life. The following discusses what a sponsor is, how to be one, and how to find one.

The BB's Chapter 7 "Working With Others" shares, from the personal experience of the first recovered alcoholics, specific directions for approaching and communicating with people who have a drinking problem and who may (or may not) want to do something about it. These are very practical suggestions about how to help those suffering with addiction. Also read BB Chapter 10 "To Employers," especially pages 140–145. These suggestions adapt well to dealing with sponsees.

Nowhere in Chapter 7—nor in the entire BB—is "sponsor" used. A book from Hazelden on sponsorship suggests the Oxford Group used the term to denote a person who brought a new person to a meeting for the first time and who took responsibility for both their personal character and group orientation. This concept carried over into AA. Bill referred to Ebby as his sponsor; Bill D. (third member of AA) referred to Bob as his sponsor. A review of early AA history shows that a sponsor would:

- Vouch for another to the hospital that the bill would be paid

- Bring the newcomer to a meeting and show them the ropes

- Take Step Three with the newly sober person
- Hear their Step Five and guide them through their Step Nine.

Since then, sponsorship has changed. AA's General Service Office has published an excellent pamphlet on sponsorship. All AA history and AA literature make it quite clear: this person is not a teacher, preacher, parent, banker, employer, or disciplinarian. In fact, Bill was quite clear that there are only two disciplines in AA: alcohol and God. If you're not surrendering to one, you're surrendering to the other.

The BB does describe the prerequisites, attitude, and the actions of sponsorship, though, without using the word specifically:

> *"But the ex-problem drinker who has found this solution, who is properly armed with facts about himself, can generally win the entire confidence of another alcoholic in a few hours. Until such an understanding is reached, little or nothing can be accomplished." (BB page 18)*

"That a man who is making the approach has had the same difficulty, that he obviously knows what he is talking about, that his whole deportment shouts at the new prospect that this is a man with a real answer, that he has no attitude of Holier Than Thou, nothing whatever except the sincere desire to be helpful; that there are no fees to pay, no axes to grind, no people to please, no lectures to be endured—these are conditions we have found most effective. After such an approach, many take up their beds and walk again." (BB pages 18–19)

"...*properly armed with facts about himself...*" My sponsor suggested this means that when an individual has completed Steps Four and Five they are eligible to be a sponsor. Before completing these two steps (where we begin to have a spiritual experience—page 75) we are not carrying the message, but may be transmitting the disease!

As we pointed out earlier, we sponsor (help) others in order to enlarge our own spiritual life (BB page 14) and immunize ourselves from our own spiritual malady. (BB page 89)

A sponsor is a person who has what you want and is willing to walk the path of recovery with you. This is a person who enjoys their own sobriety and who really cares about you, your life, and your recovery. This is a person in whom you have absolute and total confidence. You can discuss your problems, reveal your embarassing secrets, and be transparent. A sponsor is a person who has time and is willing to take time to be a sounding board or source of accountability. A sponsor is a guide to how AA works (meetings, literature, service) and especially helps with the work of the Twelve Steps. A sponsor listens and shares their experience.

A sponsor is:

Non-judgmental	Compassionate
Non-competitive	Open
Inclusive	Encouraging
Patient	Understanding
Humble	Confidential.

At the same time, a sponsor ought to be rigorous about principles and willing to tell you the truth and hold you accountable. A sponsor cares enough to be willing to hurt your feelings. A sponsor is not personally or emotionally invested in your recovery, but will be totally available to support it.

> A sponsor is a person whose reality makes God's unreality impossible
>
> - paraphrased from Thomas Merton

When looking for a sponsor, I suggest prayer and then paying particular attention to the following:

1. Do they walk like they talk?

2. Do they have a sponsor, home group, knowledge of the BB?

3. Have they worked all the Steps and completed Step Nine?

4. Do they go to meetings and have service commitments?

5. Most of all, are they enjoying their sobriety?

This is not about finding a friend, a companion to hang out with, a playmate. This may indeed happen, but it will be the result of the time spent and evolution of this relationship over time.

Interview the person you think you might want to select as a sponsor. Discuss your expectations; ask them theirs. A sponsor is <u>not</u>:

Social worker	Employer
Spiritual director	Lawyer
Guru	Accountant
"Arbiter of sex conduct" (BB page 69)	Therapist
Disciplinarian	Minister.

A sponsor helps you discern the difference between principles and personalities, between your will and God's will. It is a person who has enough information and experience to guide you along your version of the path they themselves have walked.

A sponsor is one who wants you to have your own experience—not theirs! They are the lantern that shines the light of their experience on the path they have walked so you can have your own experience. A sponsor is not the light!

My sponsor asked me to call him every day and tell him what I was thinking, feeling, and doing. It was the beginning of training me to be fully transparent and accountable. It took me out of isolation and began integrating me into the community of the human race.

There are many styles of sponsorship based on the myriad of personalities:

Directive	vs.	Non-directive
Rigid	vs.	Loose
Harsh	vs.	Soft
Focused = head	vs.	Focused = emotion.

There is no right way; no wrong way. Perhaps the middle way of balance is the most effective. We need to remember that to be helpful is our primary motive, goal, and attitude.

Regular contact is important. That may mean daily or weekly. I suggest a minimum of a weekly telephone call and an actual face-to-face meeting at least once a month.

Those you may sponsor are not medals to wear, or objects to be possessed. It is better to stay detached in order to stay objective, while caring deeply for their personal and spiritual welfare. However, don't protect them from experiencing the consequences of their actions. Usually, subjects such as religion, politics, medical and psychological opinions/advice should be avoided—they are outside issues to recovery.

I have never fired someone I sponsored. Their recovery is their business. My job is to be available, to tell the truth, and to be helpful when asked. I maintain their anonymity and purposely don't keep count or gather them together (this may build cult, not community; it may foster exclusivity, not inclusivity).

> The 12 & 12 suggests that "we are children of chaos." When we enter into another's chaos, so that they know they are not alone, we are set free from our own chaos.

I once asked my guide at what point you stop taking on sponsees. He responded that was God's business. He just made his time available. When asked to be a sponsor or step-guide, he responded: I currently have other commitments, but I'll be available later, then we can begin the process."

My experience is that the more I pay attention to my relationship with God (Step Eleven) and my service to others (Step Twelve) the more my life flourishes in all areas: personal sense of well-being, relationship with spouse and family, success at work, financial security. It is counter-intuitive and certainly counter-cultural, but the spiritual axiom is absolutely true. Based on my personal experience: the more I give away, the more I have.

This is Good News! And St. Augustine said wherever you go, preach the Good News—and if necessary, use words!

Rabbi Heschel exclaimed: "We are either servents of the sacred or slaves of evil."

Arun Gandhi (in the spirit of his grandfather the Mahatma) said: "We must live what we want others to learn; we must become the change we seek; we cannot help everyone but we must help someone."

The 12 & 12, in Step Eleven, contains the Prayer of St. Francis. This is a prayer ...

- of turning, of being turned

- from self-centeredness to other-centeredness

- of personal conversion

- of spiritual transformation

- of being awakened

- of being brought to life

- of being restored to our humanity

- of being brought to our Divinity.

Listen to this prayer's request for the transforming work of the Healing Spirit of the Universe:

"Lord, make me a channel of thy peace;

That where there is hatred, I may bring love;

That where there is wrong, I may bring the spirit of forgiveness;

That where there is discord, I may bring harmony;

That where there is error, I may bring truth;

That where there is doubt, I may bring faith;

That where there is despair, I may bring hope;

That where there are shadows, I may bring light;

That where there is sadness, I may bring joy.

Lord, grant that I may seek rather to comfort than to be comforted;

To understand, than to be understood;

To love, than to be loved.

For it is by self-forgetting that one finds;

It is by forgiving that one is forgiven;

It is by dying that one awakens to eternal life.

Amen."

The problem is our personal powerlessness. The solution is for us to find a Power other than ourselves or any other human power. The foundation stone of our spiritual life is our turning (or willingness to be turned) to OTHER and to others—in love and service.

In 1940 Father Ed Dowling, SJ (a Catholic priest in the Society of Jesus religious order) traveled from St. Louis to New York to meet Bill Wilson late one winter evening. Father Ed had read the book "Alcoholics Anonymous," published in 1939. He sensed some parallels, in terms of process and purpose, with the "Spiritual Exercises of St. Ignatius" written by the founder of the Society of Jesus (Jesuits) in the 12th century. He asked if Bill had read the "Exercises" or was acquainted with its author. Bill said he had never heard of it or St. Ignatius of Loyola. Father Dowling was delighted with this response.

They talked most of the night and discovered they were kindred souls. Father Dowling became Bill's spiritual adviser and confidante until Father Ed's death in 1960.

The conversation ended that night in 1940 with Father Dowling saying Bill had a special force inside him. He told Bill that this gift had never before been on this earth and would never again appear. It was up to him (Bill Wilson) to manifest this gift as his particular contribution to society. His gift was unique and personal. He was responsible to make a decision to nourish and use this gift for the benefit of humanity. It was up to him whether or not to respond and to manifest his destiny.

This is true for each of us. We are like individual fingerprints, each with a unique configuration of talents—our gift ... one special talent for ministering to our community. Each of us has one invitation to be of service in a way only we can contribute. It is up to us to discern what that one talent is, to nurture it, and to allow it to manifest as our own source of healing in the community we are called to serve.

Vocation comes from the Latin *"vocare"* meaning to be called, to be invited. Jim Wallis (minister and social activist) defines our individual vocation as the place where our unique gift meets the crushing need of humanity. He quotes Lisa Sullivan (author): "We are the one we have been waiting for."

Addressing the problem and solution of Post Traumatic Stress Syndrome, Judith Herman MD suggests to those seeking healing: transform the experience of personal brokenness by making it the basis for social action. This is the way to transcend it—by making it a gift to others. Our brokenness is redeemed when it becomes the source of our life's ministry (paraphrased from "Trauma and Recovery").

Our talent is the invitation; our service is the response.

In 1955 the World Service Conference adopted the principle of personal responsibility:

"When anyone, anywhere, reaches out for help,

I want the hand of AA always to be there.

And for that

I am responsible."

Summary

Purpose	Carry the Message; Practice the Principles
Instructions	Read and highlight:

    1. BB Chapter 7 (pages 89–103)

    2. Step Twelve in the 12 & 12.

Process	List the specific instructions for helping others.
Experience	Noticing the more we pay attention to helping others, the more our personal life flourishes; the results are disproportionate to effort.
Result	Build a useful, purpose-driven life, with a deep sense of self-worth and personal meaning.
Promise	Being restored to our humanity, with a place in our community.

Reflection Questions

1. Have I experienced a change in my thinking, feeling, and behavior?

2. Am I willing to share my life daily to help those I encounter?

3. What are my gifts of ministry to others? What's my invitation to serve?

4. Do I successfully manage balance in helping others, personal self-care, relationships, and work?

5. How can I improve my balance?

6. Do I operate on principles before personalities?

7. Do my behavior, demeanor, and attitude transmit the disease or the message?

8. Do I pray to be useful?

Meditation

My Spiritual Life: A Path of Service

This is the pilgrim's journey: a passage from the way of the child, self-centered and self-obsessed; a passage to other-centeredness— a relationship with:

- The Source of Power, the Spirit of the Universe underlying the totality of things
- Our community of human beings with whom we share this journey.

Wisdom is seeing as God sees and living in harmony with God's will; we take responsibility for our:

- Thoughts
- Feelings
- Behavior
- Lives.

We invite the Wisdom Spirit to enter our lives to change our:

- Desert of loneliness to a garden of solitude
- Outward-reaching craving to an inward-reaching search
- Fearful clinging to fearless service.

Underneath all is abiding, Creative Energy.
Everything is a manifestation of Divinity.
We are the pinnacle: image and likeness; knowledge and action; intellect and will.
We are all connected.
We are all community.
We are a sacred and holy people.
We are all God manifesting.

Awakening:
A Summary of the Step Process

The Twelve-Step process is engaged in primarily as the solution to addiction (substances, behaviors and processes). It is now my personal experience that it is an effective process for anyone seeking a spiritual way of life – a way of deep and lasting personal transformation. Usually it is a slow process, not a dramatic event.

Step One in this process requires some experience of personal powerlessness.

The actual solution to the problem of personal powerlessness is finding and establishing a relationship with a Power other than ourselves (other than any human power) —to find Power and to be empowered.

We establish (or re-establish) a relationship with Power:

Step Two   We first make *conscious* contact and become aware that we are always in *constant* contact; (God is our Creator, Source, and Sustainer)—a decision that is an act of faith.

Step Three   We decide to have a committed relationship, surrendering both our will and our lives to the care of God.

Then we establish (or re-establish) a relationship with ourselves:

Step Four	We see the solution to resentment, fear, and dishonesty (especially about sex) is turning to God in prayer and turning to others in service.
Step Five	We get to know God better by revealing ourselves to another human being.
Steps Six & Seven	We learn the impediments to our spiritual growth can be removed (or at least mitigated) by turning to "our Creator" so that we can be useful by being re-created.

The next phase is the establishment (or re-establishment) of our relationships with others:

Steps Eight & Nine	We clean up our relationships with people, living or dead, so that we are able to live a purpose-driven life; "Our real purpose ... to fit ourselves to be of maximum service to God and the people about us." (BB page 77)
Step Ten	We continue the formula for emotional sobriety, first *turning* to God through prayer (fostering OTHER-centeredness) because we're

powerless over our character defects, then *turning* our thoughts to helping someone (fostering other-centeredness).

Then we begin to live this way of OTHER/other-centered life:

Step Eleven   We improve our conscious contact with God so that we become better informed and more empowered to take action to live on purpose and in service.

Step Twelve   We enlarge our spiritual life through service and practicing these principles.

There appears to be a natural rhythm to the step process. This may be based on the two ingredients that make us specifically human: mind and will. First we name it (know with our mind) and then we take action (decide with our will).

Step One is an action—we concede to our innermost self that we are powerless. It is an inevitable response based on a deep connection to our actual experience. We implode into hopelessness, a realization that we are truly doomed. We name this state—powerlessness.

Step Two: with our will we decide (an action) to name "It"—Power.

Step Three: with our will we decide (an action) to have a relationship with "It" and name that relationship (such as Creator) and name that action—surrender.

Step Four: we name the obstacles in us to this relationship with "It"—spiritual malady and its manifestations.

Step Five: we take the action of "confession" to have these obstacles removed and to begin a spiritual experience of "It."

Step Six: we name the way these obstacles show up as defects in our character.

Step Seven: we acknowledge our powerlessness through taking the action of prayer.

Step Eight: we name the harms done to others which block us from "It".

Step Nine: we attempt to change the way we behave and to repair (actions) the damage to others.

Step Ten: we continue to name and have removed those things which block us from "It."

Step Eleven: we meditate to:

- Grow in consciousness of "It"
- Absorb "It"
- Be absorbed by "It"
- Become "It."

Step Twelve: we name our service to others as our life's work—to perfect and enlarge our relationship with "It."

Our rhythm is to name and take action. This is life's dance. This process is the mysterious alchemy both for personal transformation and for bringing healing to the world about us.

This process parallels the natural healing process described by Judith Herman MD (psychiatrist) in "Trauma and Recovery" for the recovery of severely psychologically damaged individuals. "Recovery is based upon the empowerment of the survivor and the creation of new connections. Recovery can take place only within the context of relationships." This recreates "... the basic capacities for trust, autonomy, initiative, competence, identity and intimacy."

The Twelve-Step process suggests that we turn to another as a guide (Steps One through Nine). Step Five requires that we seek the intimacy (into-me-you-see) of a confidante/confessor. Steps Ten, Eleven, and Twelve describe a personal submission of our will to constant evaluation, improved conscious contact, and consistent thought and action in service of others. Thus, our self-destructive mantra of "*my* will be done" is changed to the self-transcending mantra of "*Thy* will be done"—a slow evolution of self, produced by a series of acts contrary to our natural inclination of self-will.

Our problem is powerlessness, and we are given power. Our problem is isolation, and we are given community. Before recovery, we have been subjected to a vicious cycle of personal disintegration (within and without). With recovery, we have been granted a grace-filled journey of personal integration (within and without).

We are restored to our individual humanity and our global community. We get sick by ourselves; we heal in the company of others by being of service.

— STAYING AWAKE —

Journey of Freedom ...

Union and Communion

A Prayer

"It helps, now and then,

"to step back and take the long view.

The Kingdom is not only beyond our efforts,

it is even beyond our vision.

We accomplish in our lifetime only a tiny fraction of

the magnificent enterprise that is God's world.

Nothing we do is complete,

which is another way of saying that

the Kingdom always lies beyond us.

No statement says all that should be said,

no prayer fully expresses our faith.

No confession brings perfection,

no person or process brings wholeness.

No program fully accomplishes

the complete mission.

No set of goals and objectives includes everything.

That is what we are about.

We plant the seeds that one day will grow.   (con't)

We water seeds already planted,

knowing that they hold future promise.

We lay a foundation that will need further development.

We provide yeast that produces effects far beyond our
capabilities.

We cannot do everything,

and there is a sense of liberation in realizing that.

This enables us to do something,

and do it very well.

It may be incomplete, but it is a beginning,

a step along the way,

an opportunity for Grace to enter and do the rest.

We may never see the end results,

but that is the difference between

the master builder and the work.

We are workers, not master builders;

ministers, not messiahs.

We are prophets of a future that is not our own.

Amen."

—Archbishop Oscar Romero

— STAYING AWAKE —

So now what?

We've identified our problem: self-centeredness—self-will over which we are powerless.

We've identified our solution: OTHER/other-centeredness — to seek, establish, and enlarge a personal, effective relationship with Power.

This is a process of discovery that Power is already fully present deep within us, and awakening to awareness is the journey. By our willingness to respond to Grace, and our recognition that our very willingness is itself a Grace, we submit to a simple process that is not easy, yet takes us to a place we've never been. We didn't even know it existed. The results are disproportionate to our efforts. Yet, our efforts are required to sustain and enlarge it.

The Christian tradition, articulated by St. John of the Cross, suggests there are three stages to this spiritual evolution:

- Purgative: where we're detached from bondage: physical/mental and especially spiritual

- Illuminative: where Light begins to show us our darkness; that very darkness becomes the Light that allows us to name and be rid of our negative attachments and

illumines the path —a positive attachment to the Light: en-light-enment

- Unitive: where we become progressively aware of
our Source and our one-ness with "It,"
an ever-growing and over-riding yearning to realize what is already the only
Reality and that we *are* already "It."

The Buddhist tradition uses different words to describe a similar process, The Four Noble Truths:

- Life is suffering

- Suffering comes from attachments

- The solution is detachment

- Detachment is accomplished by the Eight-Fold Path of Enlightenment ...

Right view	Right livelihood
Right thought	Right effort
Right speech	Right mindfulness
Right behavior	Right concentration.

Similarly, the Twelve Steps of Alcoholics Anonymous represent a process of spiritual awakening. Their real advantage is that they are a specific method for producing this personal transformation—a change in the way a person thinks, feels, and behaves—done to the person, not by the person. It is a precise method without dogma; never exclusive but totally inclusive of all religious orientations or even no religious orientation. I have never seen this Twelve-Step process fail to produce a personal spiritual awakening when each step is thoroughly applied and all Twelve Steps are carefully completed.

Twelve-Step spirituality can be summarized:

- Trust God
- Clean house
- Help others.

The overall spiritual transformation itself is simple to explain and easy to understand, but difficult to do with consistency and rigorous self-honesty. We must remember that the goal is not attaining perfection. We need to compassionately embrace our own imperfect humanity and have confidence that the willingness to seek is enough. It is in the very seeking that we find and, indeed, are found. It is a path to the Light that we eventually discover *is* the Light. It is a path not of perfection but of progress; it is a path not of perfection but of enlightenment. It is indeed a spirituality of imperfection (Ernest Kurtz).

The spiritual malady is the universal human condition; the spiritual awakening is the historical human experience. Addiction (to substances and/or to self) is the downward spiral; spirituality is the upward spiral.

"God's gift to us is our life. We are born to unwrap this package. At death the package is finally unwrapped and opened. God delights in our delight in seeing that the gift is God Itself" (paraphrase of Jim Finley—retreat notes).

This is the spiritual process of awakening.

All non-human creation functions perfectly according to natural law:

- Rocks are inert and lie still

- Flowers grow where planted

- Animals roam for survival.

Humans, on the other hand, are:

- Negatively judgmental (of self and others) and given to ignorance

- Extremely willful, deciding everything with the self-centered motives of an inherently flawed will.

Our sin (a term from archery to describe missing the mark) is the use of our ability to say NO to God and the natural laws of the Universe. Our sanctity is the use of our ability to say YES and sing that one song—the Uni-verse.

Plato speculated that the Universe is God made flesh. All true seekers have speculated that in order to know and experience this, purification is necessary.

Purification happens by the death of our:

- Physical attachments

- Moral deviations

- Mental distractions

- Spirit of willfulness.

Through naming the impediments of self and having them removed we are being prepared by Spirit to be filled with the maximum that Source can possibly communicate of Self. This is the enlightenment journey—letting go of the false self (a humbling and painful process) and the putting on of the real Self (a gradual process of divinization).

Suffering is the invitation to transformation. Most of us find it easier to talk about our spiritual life and our spiritual principles than to live them. Authentic spirituality is not about more information, it is about more transformation.

Ken Wilber, philosopher/author, suggests there are several markers of transformation (of enlightenment)—measurable, objective behaviors. At the same time that they reveal spiritual evolution, they also precipitate and foster it. He counsels an Integral Practice, an holistic approach. For maximum results, each of us is encouraged to develop and maintain a consistent practice of caring for our:

- Body: exercise and nutrition

- Mind: information and stimulation

- Will: prayer and meditation

- Shadow: therapy and service.

Most wisdom teachers counsel:

- Learn to enjoy solitude

- Talk less but more meaningfully

- Have a guide who shows you the path and holds you accountable for your commitment

- Practice regular meditation

- Develop a passionate commitment to anonymous service.

The sun shining through a glass window illuminates the glass itself if it has smudges and smears. However, to the extent the glass is clean/clear, the glass cannot be seen. The window is transparent and allows the sun to be experienced without distraction. The glass is anonymous.

Perhaps when your anonymous service to others becomes more important than your personal experience of enlightenment, you have experienced enlightenment!

Another set of markers to evaluate the reality of our personal transformation (death of the false self) may be the following reported changes resulting from near death experiences ("Denial of Death," Ernest Becker):

- Live in the present, with deep confidence, decreased interest in material things, and increased interest in spiritual life

- Enjoy solitude

- Feel a sense of purpose to life, a sense of wonder/gratitude

- Perceive the world as a seamless garment of persons—interconnectedness

- Acknowledge a real sense of community

- Be consumed by compassion for others.

To paraphrase G. K. Chesterton: spirituality (sobriety of the body, mind, and will) has not been tried and found wanting; spirituality has been found difficult and left mostly untried.

Thomas Keating suggests ("Human Condition") that there are two great questions, and two possible answers:

Q: Where am I?

A: I am always in the presence of a loving God.

Q: Who am I?

A: I am the Love of God manifesting without conditions. I am the result of Love's excess and overflow. I am unconditional Love; I am the word of God spoken.

Therefore, this is my practice:

- Meditation/Wisdom

    I have listened deeply to Self: thus, to my true self

- Service/Compassion

    I listen deeply to you; we share in the experience of being listened to ... and we are all set free.

Our awakening is the realization that our infidelities to God do not create an impediment to God's love for us. God's love is unconditional.

Our awakening is our growing compassion for ourselves (and others) with the realization that, over time, there will be little improvement in the nature and frequency of our infidelities.

Our awakening is our growing commitment to our spiritual practice despite these realizations.

—reflections from a Jim Finley retreat

Willingness to not run away when we don't know where to go or what to do is our spiritual practice. Hope is taking the action in spite of the evidence and then watching the evidence change. Hope is seeing God in the messiness of our lives (more Jim Finley).

My personal transformation has been a profound experience that began in 1988 and continues to evolve. Human words are so inadequate to describe this experience and the resulting perception of reality. My words could be judged vague or dreamy—I'd like to believe they reveal a poetic insight.

> My self and Self, actually, are not different,
> Although I am not God, I come from, am
> sustained by, and will evolve into realized
> union with God.
>
> Knowing self, Self is my journey;
>
> Loving self, Self is my path.

In this life, pain is inevitable; this is reality. However, suffering is optional; depends on our attitude toward reality. We're meant to enjoy life, not endure it. Done correctly, we don't just survive, we thrive.

Are you doing time, or are you living life?

Millions in this world are dying from untreated addiction of one kind or another. Millions more in this world are suffering because they are somehow connected to someone dying from their various addictions. Most of those dying millions and suffering millions would eagerly embrace a spiritual way of life if they only knew about it and the solutions it provides.

> Addictions block the Sunlight of the Spirit.

Self-will is the origin of each individual's personal suffering and the ultimate cause of the chaos in the world.

> "Spirituality in the broadest, most inclusive sense, is the individual's and, therefore, humanity's only salvation."
>
> —(Twerski, *The Spiritual Self*)

Ken Wilber suggests in "Integral Spirituality" that organized religion may be the answer. Since at least 70% of the world's population belong to some form of religion, it can become the escalator to experience spirituality. Religion can be the mechanism for the transformation of each person to become fully human and realize Divinity.

However, and unfortunately, most organized religions have just enough words to block us from having a spiritual awakening.

God's only job description is to give God away completely so that others may become OTHER. The role of organized religion is to foster an environment that supports this effort and precipitates this result. It provides the inspiration, shines the Light on the path, and facilitates personal deification: a return to conscious union with Source. Religion is not the goal, it is the path.

It is patent idolotry to become too focused on any particular religion as *the* way. Religion is not the destination. Religion is the finger that points to God. However, all too many people get distracted and lost (without being aware of their distraction or of being lost). They fall prey to the all-too-human tendency to lock onto and institutionalize the method and tools; they unwittingly fossilize the path that shows the way. They begin to worship the pointing finger.

It is truly the ultimate ironic scandal when religion obscures and is an impediment to authentic spirituality, when membership in religion becomes a substittute for union with God.

How we see is what we see. Our view of reality is upside down. We need a new pair of glasses. We need a new mantra. "Thy kingdom come" requires that "my kingdom(s) go."

"The purpose of our personal enlightment is not that we transcend the world but that we transform the world" (Andrew Cohen, publisher of "What is Enlightenment?").

What is your perspective?

- The Universe is unfriendly and we are condemned to react in order to survive.

or

- The Universe is friendly and we are invited to respond in order to flourish.

YOU CHOOSE!! This power of choice is the ultimate dignity of the human being.

My choice is that we are the People of God. We have a common origin, a common path, and a common destiny. This is a fraternal journey toward a transcendent goal. And the journey is the destination. This is Good News! (paraphrase from "Letters to Contemplatives," William Johnson)

Mahatma Gandhi said we must become the change we seek (our personal transformation); we must live what we want others to learn (our unique ministry of world transformation).

The paradoxes of the Twelve-Step process are:

1. We are powerless and when we surrender— we acquire Power.

2. We are always in constant contact, but must each day foster conscious contact with God.

3. We sit powerless in the presence of Power to acquire Power.

---

4. When we sit to absorb Power: we are absorbed into Power.

5. We are turned to Divinity when we turn in service to humanity.

6. In order to keep "It," we must give "It" away.

7. Our personal lives flourish disproportionately to the time we spend in meditation (OTHER) and in service (other).

8. We already are that which we are looking for; but we must keep looking to become aware that we have found "It" and that we are "It."

Please ...

- Take the time and effort to experience this process for your own personal development. Enlightenment is available to each of us —and we deserve "It"

- Continue to foster your own spiritual life—staying awake and growing in consciousness—consistently, one day at a time

- Reveal, through your actions, the seed of this message of hope, this process of transformation, these wonderful promises of a flourishing life to your community. *Be* the Good News!

Remember—when you *do* better you'll eventually think better and feel better.

Trust that the Spirit will water the ground, the Light will open the seed, and the harvest will be plentiful.

NAMASTÉ: The God in me greets the God in you!

Summary

Reflection Questions

1. What is my underlying motive for taking this action?

2. Does this action improve my consciousness?

3. Does this action improve my effectiveness for serving others?

4. Is this action the simplest solution?

5. Is this action necessary?

6. How am I manifesting in the world?

7. What is my gift?

8. What is my invitation?

9. Is this action compatible with my vision of God's will; my gift; my invitation; my life's purpose?

Meditation

A Vision of the Future

Healing Spirit:

Let all that has divided us merge—and let compassion be wedded to power.

Let softness come to a world that is harsh and unkind.

Let both men and women be gentle yet strong.

Let no person be subject to another's will.

Let the greed of some give way to the needs of many.

Let all share equally in the earth's abundance.

Let all care for the sick and the weak and the old—let all nourish the young.

Let all cherish life's creatures—let all live in harmony with each other and the earth.

Let everywhere be called Eden once again.

—Paraphrase of poem by   Judy Chicago

Final Prayer

Healing Wisdom Spirit

I am willing to be taken to a place I don't even know exists ...

- Rend the veil so that I may see

- Remove the wax so that I may hear

- Blow open my mind so that I not just see what I know, but know what I see

- Purify my heart so that I may Love as You do—a real desire to be self-giving

- Instill in me a deep trust so that I'll respond to Your invitation

and take the right actions.

And in Your Goodness, shield me from the knowledge of my transcendence so that I'll remain humbly dependent on your Grace.

Final Meditations

God does not Love us because we are good;

we are Loved because God is good.

We are not Loved because of what we do;

we are Loved because of who we are.

God cannot Love us any more

no matter what we do or don't do;

God cannot Love us any less

no matter what we do or don't do;

God is Source

We come from, are sustained by,

and evolve toward awareness of our union with this Source.

Final Meditations

Finding Self

God by nature Is; by necessity becomes.

Self giving is self-received.

God is powerless to not create;

we are powerless as created,

except to seek that creating Power.

God is Everything; thus, we are too!

One with, but not identical to.

Our separation comes from self—our isolation.

Unification is our journey in Self—our invitation.

Losing self is a process of finding Self—our transformation

In giving self we become Self—our community.

To live by God's will restores me.

To love in God's presence restores us.

My response is: THANK YOU!

My answer is: YES!!

APPENDICIES

APPENDIX A

What Is a Personality Disorder?

From Diagnostic and Statistical Manual of Mental Disorders, 4th edition, 1994, commonly referred to as DSM-IV, of the American Psychiatric Association. European countries use the diagnostic criteria of the World Health Organization.

An enduring pattern of inner experience and behavior that deviates markedly from the expectation of the individual's culture, is pervasive and inflexible, has an onset in adolescence or early adulthood, is stable over time, and leads to distress or impairment.

A personality disorder is a pattern of deviant or abnormal behavior that the person doesn't change even though it causes emotional upsets and trouble with other people at work and in personal relationships. It is not limited to episodes of mental illness, and it is not caused by drug or alcohol use, head injury, or illness. There are about a dozen different behavior patterns classified as personality disorders by DSM-IV. All the personality disorders show up as deviations from normal in one or more of the following:

- Cognition—perception, thinking, and interpretation of oneself, other people, and events
- Affectivity—emotional responses (range, intensity, liability, appropriateness)
- Interpersonal functions
- Impulsivity.

Narcissistic Personality Disorder (NPD) — indicators are:

1. An exaggerated sense of self-importance (e.g., exaggerates achievements and talents, expects to be recognized as superior without commensurate achievements); grandiosity.

2. preoccupation with fantasies of unlimited success, power, brilliance, beauty, or ideal love

3. belief of being "special"; only can be understood by, or should associate with, other special or high-status people (or institutions)

4. Requiring excessive admiration

5. Sense of entitlement

6. Selfishness in taking advantage of others to achieve their own ends

7. Lacking empathy

8. Envy of others or belief that others envy them

9. Behaviors or attitudes that are arrogant, haughty, patronizing, or contemptuous

Appendix B

History Pre-AA

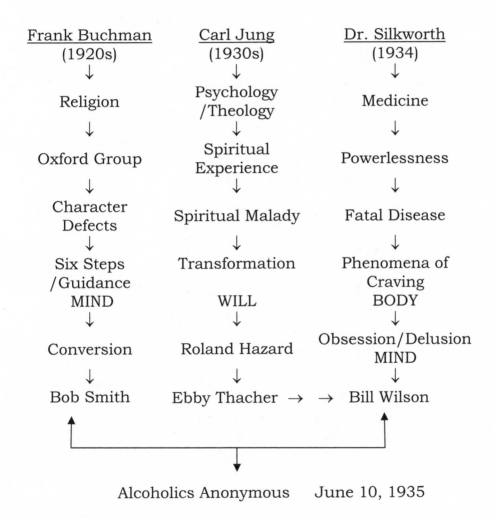

Frank Buchman (1920s)	Carl Jung (1930s)	Dr. Silkworth (1934)
↓	↓	↓
Religion	Psychology /Theology	Medicine
↓	↓	↓
Oxford Group	Spiritual Experience	Powerlessness
↓	↓	↓
Character Defects	Spiritual Malady	Fatal Disease
↓	↓	↓
Six Steps /Guidance MIND	Transformation	Phenomena of Craving BODY
↓	WILL ↓	↓
Conversion	Roland Hazard	Obsession/Delusion MIND
↓	↓	↓
Bob Smith	Ebby Thacher →	→ Bill Wilson

Alcoholics Anonymous   June 10, 1935

Appendix C

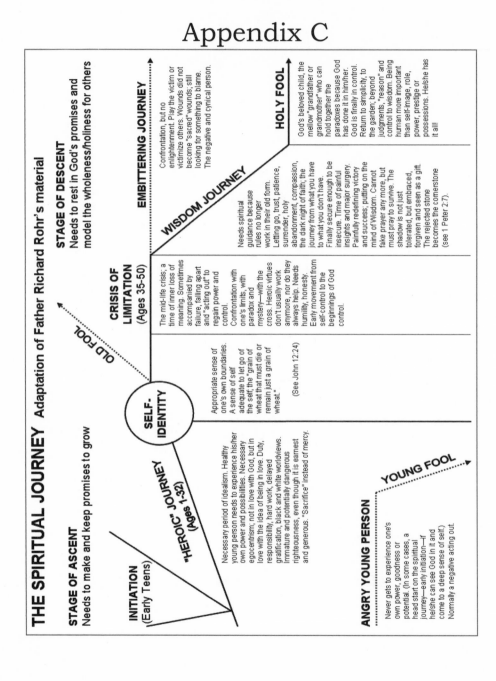

THE SPIRITUAL JOURNEY Adaptation of Father Richard Rohr's material

STAGE OF ASCENT
Needs to make and keep promises to grow

STAGE OF DESCENT
Needs to rest in God's promises and
model the wholeness/holiness for others

INITIATION
(Early Teens)

"HEROIC" JOURNEY
(Ages 1-32)

WISDOM JOURNEY

EMBITTERING JOURNEY

OLD FOOL

YOUNG FOOL

HOLY FOOL

SELF-IDENTITY

CRISIS OF LIMITATION
(Ages 35-50)

Necessary period of idealism. Healthy young person needs to experience his/her own power and possibilities. Necessary egocentrism; not in love with God, but in love with the idea of being in love. Duty, responsibility, hard work, delayed gratification, black and white worldviews. Immature and potentially dangerous righteousness, even though it is earnest and generous. "Sacrifice" instead of mercy.

Appropriate sense of one's own boundaries. A sense of self adequate to let go of the self; the "grain of wheat that must die or remain just a grain of wheat."

(See John 12:24)

The mid-life crisis; a time of inner loss of meaning. Sometimes accompanied by failure, falling apart and "acting out" to regain power and control. Confrontation with one's limits, with paradox and mystery—with the cross. Heroic virtues don't usually work anymore, nor do they always help. Needs humility, honesty. Early movement from self-control to the beginnings of God control.

Needs spiritual guidance because rules no longer work in their old form. Letting go, trust, patience, surrender, holy abandonment, compassion, the dark night of faith; the journey from what you have to what you don't have. Finally secure enough to be insecure. Time of painful insights and major surgery. Painfully redefining victory and success; putting on the mind of Wisdom. Cannot fake prayer any more, but must pray to survive. The shadow is not just tolerated, but embraced, forgiven and seen as a gift. The rejected stone becomes the cornerstone (see 1 Peter 2:7).

Confrontation, but no enlightenment. Play the victim or victimize others. Wounds did not become "sacred" wounds; still looking for something to blame. The negative and cynical person.

God's beloved child, the mellow "grandfather or grandmother" who can hold together the paradoxes because God has done it in him/her. God is finally in control. Return to simplicity, to the garden; beyond judgments, "reason" and control to wisdom. Being human more important than self-image, role, power, prestige or possessions. He/she has it all!

ANGRY YOUNG PERSON

Never gets to experience one's own power, goodness or potential. (In some cases, a head start on the spiritual journey—early initiation—if he/she can see God in it and come to a deep sense of self.) Normally a negative acting out.

APPENDIX D

January 30, 1961
Kusnacht-Zurich
Seestrasse 228

Mr. William G. Wilson
Alcoholics Anonymous
Box 459 Grand Central Station
New York 17, N.Y.

Dear Mr. Wilson,

Your letter has been very welcome indeed.

I had no news from Roland H. anymore and often wondered what has been his fate.

Our conversation which he has adequately reported to you had an aspect of which he did not know. The reason that I could not tell him everything was that in those days I had to be exceedingly careful of what I said. I had found out that I was misunderstood in every possible way. Thus I was very careful when I talked to Roland H. But what I really thought about, was the result of many experiences with men of his kind.

His craving for alcohol was the equivalent on a low level of the spiritual thirst of our being for wholeness, expressed in mediaeval language: the union with God.(1)

How could one formulate such an insight in the language that is not misunderstood in our days?

The only right and legitimate way to such an experience is that it happens to you in reality and it can only happen to you when you walk on a path, which leads you to higher understanding. You might be led to that goal by an act of grace or through a personal and honest contact with friends, or through a higher education of the mind beyond the confines of mere rationalism. I see from your letter that Roland H. has chosen the second way, which was, under the circumstances, obviously the best one.

I am strongly convinced that the evil principle prevailing in this world leads the unrecognized spiritual need into perdition, if it is not counteracted wither by a real religious insight or by the protective wall of human community. An ordinary man, not protected by an action from above and isolated in society cannot resist the power of evil, which is called very aptly the Devil. But the use of such words arouse so many mistakes that one can only keep aloof from them as much as possible.

These are the reasons why I could not give a full and sufficient explanation to Roland H. but I am risking it with you, because I conclude from your very decent and honest letter, that you have acquired a point of view above the misleading platitudes one usually hears about alcoholism.

You see, Alcohol in Latin is "spiritus" and you use the same word for the highest religious experience as well as for the most depraving poison. The helpful formula therefore is: spiritus contra spiritum.

Thanking you again for your kind letter

     I remain
          yours sincerely
               C.J. Jung

(1) "As the hart panteth after the water brooks, so panteth my soul after thee, O God. (Psalm 42, 1)

APPENDIX E

Before you begin the worksheet write and pray a personal version of the Set Aside Prayer:

_____

Ask yourself: When I resent(ed) _____(Column One) for _____
_____ (Column Two), does /did it hurt, threaten, or interfere with my:

What is my fear?
(May be the opposite
of my **belief**)

Self-esteem (What is my deep **belief** about who I am?)
I am _____
_____   [   ]

Pride (How do I want other people to see me being treated by [insert Column
One name]_____?)
Others should see (Column One name) _____ treating me as: [   ]
_____
_____

Ambition (What do I want?)
I want _____   [   ]
_____

Security (What do I need? **Why** do I need it?)
I need _____   [   ]

Personal relations (How should family, friends or co-workers see or treat me?)
Family, friends or co-workers should always treat me as _____   [   ]
_____

Sex (gender) **relations** (What is my **belief** about men/women?)
The ideal/model man should always or is _____   [   ]
_____

The ideal/model woman should always or is _____   [   ]
_____

Pocketbook (What is the affected **value**? For example: money,
emotional security, etc.)
No one should do anything that interferes with, affects, or diminishes my
_____   [   ]
_____

Resentment Worksheet: Step Four, Column Four

Before you begin the worksheet write and pray a personal version of the Set Aside Prayer:
_____
                                                                                                    "

When I resent(ed) _____(Column One) for _____ (Column Two),
I have / had this belief about my role (from Column Three):

My perceived role (like an actor in a play= misunderstood person, betrayed spouse, abused child, etc)

_____

Is the **event** true or false? (Did it really happen?)_____

Consider: before, during and after the event that was/is the occasion for this resentment. Then **write** one
sentence answering these questions:

WHERE WAS I ... (at the time of the actual event), or **WHERE AM I...** (at present time)

1.   **Selfish? (Thinking** about myself) _____

2.   **Self-seeking? (Acting** on my own behalf) _____

3.   **Dishonest?** (Misrepresenting myself : lying by commission or omission) _____
     _____

4.   **Afraid?** (Fear of not getting what I want; or losing what I have) _____
     _____

5.   **Where am I wrong/at fault/to blame** (responsible), then and/or now? _____
     _____

6.   **What harm did I cause to this person?** (How did I specifically diminish this person?)
     a.   Physical (Body)_____
     b.   Mental (Mind)_____
     c.   Emotional (Feelings)_____
     d.   Spiritual (Relation with God) _____
     e.   Financial (Money)_____

7.   What **harm** did I cause to **other** people, in and around this relationship?   (Write name and specific
     harm)   _____
     _____

8.   List any other **fears** you have become aware of:

     _____   _____   _____   _____
     _____   _____   _____   _____

9.   List the **character defect**(s) I've become aware of while completing this worksheet:

     _____   _____   _____   _____

My real role (now, in light of the Column Four information – may be opposite of my **perceived** role at
the top of this worksheet) _____

Fear Worksheet

Name my fears	Why do I have it?	What behavior is manifest as the result of this fear?	Name the opposite of this fear? (the virtue)	What behaviour would this manifest? (the opposite of Column Three)

Sex Inventory Worksheet

Begin with writing and then praying a personal version of the Set Aside Prayer for an open mind and open heart:

_____

Review the facts - We are looking at our **motives** and actual **behavior**:

- How did the encounter or relationship begin?
- What happened?
- What is the status now, or how did it end?

Answer these questions:

1. Where had I been selfish? (Thinking about myself)

2. Where had I been dishonest? (By commission or omission)

3. Where had I been inconsiderate?

4. Whom had I hurt?

5. Did I arouse jealousy?

6. Did I arouse suspicion?

7. Did I arouse bitterness?

8. Where was I at fault?

9. What should I have done instead?

    The answer to question #9 will help you become conscious of the principles you already have but are not aware of (or the principles you want to have) that will guide your future sex motives and behavior. They will form the basis of your "sex ideal".

APPENDIX F

Character Defects Worksheet

Character Defect	What is my behavior?	What am I defending?	What is the opposite of this defect? (the virtue)	What behavior would this manifest? (the opposite of Column Two)

APPENDIX G

Prayer and Meditation Practice

Morning

Prayer

- Set-Aside Prayer
    God, please set aside everything that I think
    I know about myself, my brokenness, my
    spiritual path and you, God, for an open
    mind and a new experience of myself, my
    brokenness, my spiritual path and
    especially you, God!
- Step Three Prayer (BB pg 63)
    God, I offer myself to Thee, to build with me
    and to do with me as Thou wilt. Relieve me of
    the bondage of self, that I may better do Thy
    will. Take away my difficulties, that victory over
    them may bear witness, to those I would help,
    of Thy Power, Thy Love, and Thy Way of Life.
    May I do Thy will always!

Reading (Lectio Divina)
    Inspirational reading (Big Book, scripture, etc).

Preparation

- Is my attitude one of prayerful attention?

- What is my purpose?:

  1. To improve my *conscious contact* with God.

  2. To enhance my *usefulness* to others.

  3. To develop *humility*: makes it possible to receive God's help.

- Who is God—"As I understand Him"?:

Is God:

  1. EVERYTHING?

  2. ALL KNOWLEDGE?

  3. ALL POWER?

  4. ALL LOVE?

  5. ALL PRESENCE?

- Where is God? Do I believe God is deep down inside of me?

Meditation   Use my mind to create my vision of God's will for me

- Father, please direct my thinking; especially divorce it from motives of:

Selfishness	Resentment
Self-Seeking	Fear
Self-Pity	Dishonesty

  Please clear my thinking of wrong motives.

  Allow me to be *attentive*.

- Think   about the 24 hours ahead (*doing*)   What will I *do*?
- Consider   my plans for the day (*being*)   Who will I *be*?

- See   my vision of God's will for me today (*intent*)   What is *my* vision?

     How can I best serve You?

- Decide   to relax and take it easy; to stop struggling   What action is suggested?

Contemplation   Use my *will* to be present to the Presence of God

Allow the Spirit to guide me.

Respond from my *heart*.

Embrace the Mystery.

Be conscious of my *intention*.

Concluding Prayer

KNOWLEDGE   God, show me all through the day what my next step is to be

POWER   Give me whatever I need to take care of tasks and problems

FREEDOM   Especially free me from SELF-WILL

LOVE   Show me the way of patience, tolerance, kindliness, and love

SERVICE   Allow today's WORK to provide an opportunity to be useful and helpful. What can I do today for the person who is still suffering?

- Step Seven Prayer (BB pg 76)

  My Creator,
  I am now willing that you should have all of
  me, good and bad. I pray that you now remove
  from me every single defect of character that
  stands in the way of my usefulness to You and
  my fellows. Grant me strength as I go out from
  here to do Your bidding. Amen

Evening

Purpose   Identify and remove obstacles to the
                    Sunlight of the Spirit.

- Set-Aside Prayer
  God, please set aside everything that I think I
  know about myself, my brokenness, my
  spiritual path and you, God, for an open mind
  and a new experience of myself, my
  brokenness, my spiritual path and especially
  you, God!

- Meditation

1. CONSTRUCTIVELY review my day (without fear or favor)

  A. Was I: What *motives* were underneath my:
      1. Resentful?   Intentions?
      2. Selfish?   Thoughts?
      3. Dishonest?   Acts?
      4. Afraid?   Effort?

  B. Do I owe an apology?

  C. Have I kept something to myself which should be
      discussed with another person at once?

  D. Was I kind and loving toward all?

  E. What could I have done better?

F. Was I thinking of myself most of the time?

G. Or was I thinking of what I could do for others, of what I could pack into the stream of life?

2. Ask God's forgiveness!

3. Ask what corrective measures should be taken.

4. Thank Him for blessings received!

5. Be willing to try again tomorrow!

6. Conclude with the Prayer of St. Francis
    Lord, make me a channel of thy peace;
    That where there is hatred, I may bring love;
    That where there is wrong, I may bring the spirit of forgiveness;
    That where there is discord, I may bring harmony;
    That where there is error, I may bring truth;
    That where there is doubt, I may bring faith;
    That where there is despair; I may bring hope;
    That where there are shadows, I may bring light;
    That where there is sadness, I may bring joy.
    Lord, grant that I may seek rather to comfort than to be comforted;
    To understand, than to be understood;
    To love, than to be loved.
    For it is by self-forgetting that one finds;
    It is by forgiving that one is forgiven;
    It is by dying that one awakens to eternal life.
    Amen!

All Day

Pray for **knowledge** and **Power**:

- *PAUSE* frequently– when agitated or doubtful: ask for the right
  Thought
  or
  Action

- Many times humbly say: "Thy will be done!"

- ***THINK*** what you can **DO** for others!

BIBLIOGRAPHY

This is a list of the primary books that have influenced me; it is not an endorsement of an author's philosophy or opinion.

Anonymous   *The Cloud of Unknowing*. New York, Doubleday, 1973.

Karen Armstrong   *A History of God*. New York, Ballentine, 1993.

Dick B.   *The Good Book and The Big Book*. Kihei, HI, Paradise Research Publication, 1997.

Hamilton B.   *Twelve Step Sponsorship*. Center City, MN, Hazelden, 1996.

Melody Beattie   *Beyond Codependency :*. New York, Harper & Row, 1989.

                       Codependent No More. Center City, MN, Hazelden, 1992.

Ernest Becker   *Denial of Death*. New York, Free Press, 1973.

Cynthia Bourgeault   *Centering Prayer and Inner Awakening*. Cambridge, MA, Cowley Publications, 2004.

                       The Wisdom Way of Knowing. San Francisco, Jossey-Bass, 2003.

Patrick Brennan   *The Way of Forgiveness*. Ann Arbor, Mich, Charis/Servant Publications, 2000.

Chuck C.   *New Pair of Glasses*. Irvine, CA, New-Look Publishing, 1983.

Jean-Pierre de Caussade	*The Joy of Full Surrender.* Orleans, MA, Paraclete Press , 1986.
Jim Finley	*Christian Meditation.* San Francisco, Harper San Francisco, 2004.
	Contemplative Heart. Notre Dame, Ind, Ave Maria Press, 1978.
	Merton's Palace of Nowhere. Notre Dame, Ind, Ave Maria Press, 2003.
Robert Fitzgerald, SJ	*The Soul of Sponsorhip.* Center City, MN, Hazelden, 1995.
Emmet Fox	*Sermon on the Mount.* San Francisco, Harper San Francisco, 1992.
Viktor Frankel	*Man's Search for Meaning.* Boston, Beacon Press, 2006.
R.M. French	*The Way of the Pilgrim.* New York, Harper Collins, 1973.
Erich Fromm	*The Art of Loving.* New York, Perennial, 2000.
Kevin Griffin	*One Breath at a Time (Buddhism and the Twelve Steps).* Emmaus, Pa, Rodale / St. Martin's Press , 2004.
Ruben Habito	*Total Liberation.* Marikina, Metro Manila, Philippine, Zen Center for Oriental Spirituality, 1986.
Thích Nhất Hạnh	*Living Buddha, Living Christ.* New York, Riverhead Books, 1995.
David R. Hawkins	*Power vs. Force.* Carlsbad, CA, Hay House , 2002.
Harville Hendrix	*Getting the Love You Want.* New York, Harper Perenia, 1988.

Judith Herman	*Trauma and Recovery*. New York, BasicBooks, 1997.
Abraham Heschel	*I Asked for Wonder*. New York, Crossroads, 1983.
Karen Horney	*Neurosis and Human Growth*. New York, W.W.Norton, 1950.
William James	*Varieties of Religious Experience*. New York, Collier Book, 1961.
William Johnson	*Arise My Love*. Maryknoll, NY , Orbis , 2001.
	Mystical Theology. Maryknoll, NY , Orbis , 1995.
Keiran Kavaneugh	*The Collected Works of Saint John of the Cross*. Washington, DC, Institute of Carmelite Studies, 1995.
Thomas Keating	*Intimacy with God*. New York, Continuum, 2002.
	Invitation to Love. New York, Continuum, 2001.
	Manifesting God. New York, Lantern, 2005.
	Open Heart Open Mind. New York, Continuum, 1994.
Sam Keen	*Fire in the Belly*. New York, Bantam, 1991.
Jack Kornfield	*A Path with Heart*. New York, Bantam, 1993.
	After Ecstasy, the Laundry. New York, Bantam, 2000.

Wayne Kritsberg   *The Adult Children Of Alcoholics Syndrome.* Pompano Beach, FL, Health Communications , 1986.

Ernest Kurtz   *Not God.* Center City, MN, Hazelden, 1979.

Spirituality of Imperfection. New York, Bantam, 1992.

Brother Lawrence   *The Practice of the Presence of God.* Amberson, PA, Scroll, 2001.

Fred Luskin   *Forgive for Good.* New York, Harper Collins, 2002.

Gerald May   *Addiction and Grace.* San Francisco, Harper & Row, 1988.

Simply Sane. New York, Crossroads, 1994.

The Awakened Heart. New York, Harper Collins, 1991.

The Dark Night of the Soul. San Francisco, Harper San Francisco, 2003.

Will and Spirit. New York, Harper Collins, 1982.

Pia Melody   *Facing Codependence.* New York, Harper Collins, 1989.

Facing Love Addiction. New York, Harper Collins, 2003.

The Intimacy Factor. New York, Harper Collins, 2003.

Thomas Merton   *New Seeds of Contemplation.* New York, New Directions, 1962.

Alice Miller — *Drama of the Gifted Child.* New York, BasicBooks, 1994.

For Your Own Good. New York, Farrar Straus and Giroux, 2002.

Caroline Myss — *Entering the Castle.* New York, Free Press, 2007.

Scott Peck — *The Road Less Traveled.* New York, Touchstone, 1978.

M. Basil Pennington — *True Self/False Self.* New York, Crossroads, 2000.

Peace Pilgrim — *Her Life and Work in Her Own Words.* Santa Fe, NM , Ocean Tree, 1982.

Chogyam Trungpa Rinpoche — *Cutting Through Spiritual Materialism.* Boston , Shambhala /Random House, 1987.

Don Riso — *Understanding the Enneagram.* Boston, Houghton Mifflin, 1990.

Richard Rohr — *Everything Belongs.* New York, Crossroads, 1999.

Wild Man's Journey. Cincinnati, OH, St. Anthony's Messenger, 1992.

Don Miguel Ruiz — *The Four Agreement.* San Rafael, CA, Amber-Allen, 1997.

George Saint-Laurent — *Spirituality and World Religions.* Mountain View, CA, Mayfield, 2000.

Daniel Siegel — *Mindsight.* New York, Bantam, 2010.

The Developing Mind. New York, Guilford Press, 1999.

Shunryu Suzuki	*Zen Mind, Beginners Mind.* Boston , Weatherhill, 2006.
Eckhart Tolle	*A New Earth.* New York, Penguin, 2006.
	Stillness Speaks. Novato, CA, New World Library, 2003.
	The Power of Now. Novato, CA, New World Library, 1999.
Neal Donald Walsch	*Conversations with God (Book* . New York, G.P. Putnam, 1996.
Rick Warren	*The Purpose Driven Live.* Grand Rapids, MI, Zondervan, 2002.
Ken Wilber	*A Theory of Everything.* Boston, Shambhala, 2000.
	Integral Spirituality. Boston, Shambhala, 2006.
	The Simple Feeling of Being. Boston, Shambhala, 2004.
Marianne Williamson	*A Return to Love.* New York, Harper Collins, 1992.

ACKNOWLEDGEMENTS

My step-guides: the most important influences for my books are four men, Jerry R., Rod S., Joe H., and Mark H. who shone the light of their experience on the path they had walked, so that I could trudge it and have my own experience.

Debra Sanders: a professional editor and a spiritual woman. She was dedicated to the effective communication of the message of transformation - the goal of this book. Because she is not in a Twelve-Step program, she was able to lovingly challenge program jargon while preserving the integrity of the narrative of my personal experience.

Kate Mears: my faithful typist, methodically and patiently translated my handwritten hieroglyphics into a draft that would be word-smithed ad infinitum.

Stan M., my publisher: a CFO by day – thus the attention to detail on which I depended; a recovered alcoholic by Grace – thus his wonderful gift of understanding, not only of the mechanics of the Big Book step process, but also the spiritual intuition that comes from having had his own spiritual awakening.

And a huge thank you to all the people who have attended my workshops and retreats - for giving me the inspiration, motivation and encouragement to bring the workshop experience into print.

Also by the Author:

Twelve-Step Guide to Using the Alcoholics Anonymous Big Book:
Personal Transformation: The Promise of the Twelve-Step Process
Capizon Publishing   192 pages   ISBN 978-0-9659672-2-8

> This is a workbook that confirms the instructions of "precisely how we recovered" as outlined in AA's Big Book. Its purpose is to guide individuals to and through the Twelve Steps. It is a companion to the Big Book—a Rosetta stone that unlocks and reveals the instructions for working each of the Twelve Steps.

CDs / Tapes from Herb K's workshops and retreats
Please visit www.herbk.com for current prices and ordering information.

A Day In The Steps   (4 CDs/Tapes)
   Discussion of all Twelve Steps
   Instructions, Process, Experience, Promises

Twelve Steps: Purpose, Process & Promises   (2 CDs/Tapes)

Forgiveness: Of Others & Myself   (2 CDs/Tapes)

Step Eleven: Prayer, Meditation, Contemplation   (2 CDs/Tapes)
   A Daily Practice

Twelve-Step Spirituality   (6 CDs/Tapes)
   Step Process & Promises
   Forgiveness: Of Others & Myself
   Meditation: A Daily Practice

Meditation Workshop   (5 CDs/Tapes)
  Herb's Story
  12 Step Overview
  In Depth Discussion of Step Eleven

Step Eleven Meditations   (2 CDs/Tapes)
  Discussion and actual meditation practice
  Spiritual Journey, with 5-minute silent meditation period
  Forgiveness, with 10-minute silent meditation period

Sponsorship   (2 CDs/Tapes)
  What It Is and Isn't
  How to Sponsor
  How to Be Sponsored

Step Eleven: A Contemplative Practice   (2 CDs/Tapes)
  Review of Centering Prayer

In Contemplation of Him Who Presides Over Us All   (1 CD/Tape)
  Discussion of Step Twelve and Tradition Twelve

Twelve-Step Spirituality – Our Way of Life   (6 CDs/Tapes)
  An in-depth review of the 12-Step Process

Our Way of Life   (6 CDs/Tapes)
  Staying conscious - Steps 4, 10, 11
  Improving consciousness - Steps 2, 3, 11
  Enlarging consciousness - Steps 1, 7, 9, 12

Please visit www.herbk.com for more information.